What Are You Holding Onto That's Holding You Back?

GERRY BOYLAN

Copyright © 2010 by Gerry Boylan

Chicago Spectrum Press
4824 Brownsboro Center
Louisville, Kentucky 40207
502-899-1919

Printed in the U.S.A.

10 9 8 7 6 5 4 3 2 1

ISBN: 978-1-58374-228-0

Cover design by Gerry Boylan and Victoria Voelker

DEDICATION

Margo, my partner in life, you have opened my heart, blessed me with your presence, and gifted me with your love and wisdom.
Our grandchildren, Mikayla, Paige, Meaghan, Aoife, and Fionn, you light up my life; you make the world a sunnier place.
I prayerfully wish you joy, peace, and all the happiness you can hold.

ACKNOWLEDGMENTS

MY GRATEFUL acknowledgment and blessings go to all those who have illumined my path. As a learner, I continue to hear the whispers and echoes of my many teachers. Some names and faces have been lost in the haze of my past, and others come to mind as I ponder a word or a phrase I have just written. I would especially like to recognize the Xaverian Brothers, who mentored and nurtured me into adulthood, may your loving work continue to prosper; Jacquie Small, whose light and wisdom continue to grace me; Ram Dass, whom I have met only briefly, but whose teachings continue to inspire compassion and devotion.

To all the people who have contributed to this book, especially Sharron Aiken, for proofing; Bob Cole, whose editing skills and guiding comments have been priceless; Victoria Voelker, for her loving hand in typesetting and page design; and Margaret McIntyre-Galligher, for cover design and graphics.

My appreciation and gratitude also go to all those who have read through and commented on earlier versions of the manuscript, especially my cousin and brother in Spirit, Fred Ashley, my friend and mentor Dona Airey, and Unity Ministers Rev. Carole Mahaffey, Revs. Susan Eng-Poole and Jack Poole.

Deepest gratitude as well to:

Jesus, the Christ, who told us, "Greater things than this shall you do"; and the Christ in all of us;

The ministers and congregations of Unity of Louisville and Middletown for all your affirmation, love, and support;

The people of Twelve Step fellowships, worldwide, who continue to save and heal lives;

All my students, who have given me more than I could ever give them;

All my clients, who continue to teach me, thank you for sharing your lives;

My family and friends, whose love and support allowed me the time, space, and energy to write, and especially for Margo who not only created the spiritual and emotional space for me to work in, but also lovingly nurtured the ideas in this book as they began to take form;

And to all those who have made their stories part of my own. Thank you all.

AUTHOR'S NOTE

AT THE CONCLUSION of the second chapter, Opening to Surrender, and each following chapter there will be a meditation. You may read these exercises yourself or have someone read them to you. The first meditation will have an extended introduction and closing which you may use for all the meditations. The meditations at the end of the other chapters have a briefer introduction and closing.*

As these meditations and imageries require relaxation, do not use them when your concentration is needed for other tasks, such as driving, cooking, or the like.

I write often about my wife and grandchildren, but if there seems to be a generation missing, there is not. I do not have any children of my own. Margo was a widow with two grown children when we married. All the grandchildren began to come along after that. Her son Roger, his wife Barbara, her daughter Margaret and husband John, have become a wonderful part of my life and family. I am grateful for our relationship and for the blessing their children are to me.

A note on nuggets: What I am calling NUGGETS are simply some additional thoughts to ponder. Some will probably be more meaningful for you than others. My friend Bob Cole pointed out to me that some chapters are "more nuggetty" than others. I agree, but I decided to keep them all since every one of them has importance to me.

Many years ago I heard a story about something called a "monkey trap." Hunters would hollow out a coconut or a gourd and leave a small round opening. They would then put some sweet-smelling berries in the hollowed-out shell. With a leather thong tied at one end, the shell was firmly fastened to a tree or a stake in the ground. Monkeys would come along, be attracted by the berries, and reach in to get them. The monkey's hand, when empty, was tiny enough to squeeze into the little opening, but when the monkey's closed fist was tightly clutching the berries it proved to be too big to pull out. As frightened and as desperate as the monkey became, he never let go of the berries. All the hunter had to do was show up and bonk him on the head.

This is a book about monkey traps, and how to get your hand out.

---

*Audio recordings of the meditations are available from our Web site, http://christintraining.com.

What Are You Holding Onto

TABLE OF CONTENTS

INTRODUCTION

NOTHING LASTS forever, not even wisdom. No matter how much I have learned or how much I absorb, I want more. "Ah, this is it," I say, and then after a time the flower of knowing loses its fragrance and the nectar of certainty its sweetness. Even if the ideas and truths I have studied remain as fresh and vibrant as when I first encountered them, there is a part of me that becomes restless and dissatisfied. Although I know "the Truth is the Truth" and only its form of presentation changes, there remains a part of me that can never settle for that. There is an element of my nature that is like a little kitten, both curious and dissatisfied. It is always searching for something new and stimulating, jumping from one thing to another. This part of my personality is always messing around, looking to chase a butterfly, to swat at a dandelion, or to pretend he is frightened of the wind.

Many of us still have a shelf of self-help books at home or a list of books we must read despite the fact that we have consciously given up on finding that magic book that we thought would change our lives and our fortunes. Perhaps we have come to realize no matter how magical the book might be, the transformation we seek will always need continuing work.

I am caught between the wish to find the book which will explain it all (as well as do it all for me), and the knowing that the answers are never going to be found "out there" someplace. Added to this conflict, I continue to find myself giving into my sense of incompleteness and boredom. I am hungry for novelty. All the answers might be staring me in the face, but I am seeking the truth in a different package. I want to be stimulated and excited when I take the truth in again. My fires have grown dull, and as childish as it might seem, I need an infusion of energy. I need the challenge of another way of looking at my life. I need a spiritual booster shot. I push and I push, and I finally realize I am trying to do this all by myself. No wonder I am tired and frustrated! I am seeking God without seeking God's help. I am a hunter shooting blanks, an archer with cotton-ball arrows. All the pushing I have done has not created the spiritual stimulation I crave, but it has brought me to the brink of surrender.

"Ah, God," I pray, "here I am again, seeking an answer that is already here; searching for magic; looking for an easier, softer way. Wait a second, Lord; perhaps I am being unfair to myself. Please, teach me to accept and love myself as I am now, so that I might realize my restlessness and dissatisfaction are a mirror of my longing for You. I know there have been many times when I thought I knew what I needed, and once I got it, I realized it was not what I was after. So here I am, Lord, seeking You, but I'm in the dark here. I'm a little lost. I could use a hand. Help me; heal me; guide me. Thank You, Lord. Amen."

I stop struggling. I stop trying to control everything. I stop fighting. I stop pushing. I stop trying to figure it out. I stop. I surrender. I let go. I have surrendered enough to know that letting go is not just a step on the spiritual path, it *is* the spiritual path. I have surrendered enough that it should be an automatic response, but it is not. I have surrendered enough to be aware that it is essentially the answer to all questions on the spiritual quest, but I have a difficult time remembering that truth. I keep coming back to the place of surrender so often. When I am on the brink of hopelessness and despair, I surrender. When I am overcome with grief and sadness about a personal event or the world in general, I surrender. When I am a tired, bloody mess from banging my head against the wall, I surrender. When I find I have been seeking God without God's help, I surrender. When I experience myself wanting to love so deeply, it seems that I will burst, I surrender. Even then the questions arise: "Am I doing it right? Does it ever end? Do I ever get there? What am I surrendering? Who or what am I surrendering to? Is there any way to make it easier?" The answers to all these questions can only become known through the act of surrender itself.

I surrender to a power greater than my ego, greater than my limited sense of self, and allow myself to be immersed in peace and to be guided by God's unconditional love.

IT'S ALL ABOUT SURRENDER

I DIDN'T HAVE MUCH *of a body, and my soul seemed to be an insignificant thing, so I had to rely on a quick mind and a smart mouth. Although I was taught that God is Love, that never seemed quite true when I was being smacked on the hand with a steel ruler or yelled at for just being a kid. Quick mind and smart mouth seemed to be the only tools I could rely on. Life was not a mystery to be lived; it was a problem to be solved. Life was a monstrous thing, much bigger than me, and it was my job to figure it out so I could survive.*

Each time a change occurs in our lives, when we grieve, or make an act of faith, we surrender. Each time we forgive, or allow ourselves to see something differently, or let go of an addiction or an attachment, we surrender. Each time we go beyond the intellect into mystery; each time we are willing to give and bend a little, we surrender. In surrendering, we are open to a larger, more expansive part of ourselves that we sometimes forget exists. It is this awakening, this surrendering into a greater Self, which forms the basis and the heart of our spiritual lives.

Most of us are familiar with the marvelous story of the atheistic mountain climber who, when stranded, hanging by a single rope with nowhere to go but down, finally yells in desperation, "If there is a God up there, help me." To his ultimate surprise and astonishment an immediate reply was forthcoming. "Yes," said a thundering but kind voice, "I will help you. All you must do is let go of the rope." The startled mountain climber thought about this for a moment, and again raised his eyes to heaven and asked, "Is there anyone else up there?"

This tale is wonderfully paralleled by one from the Buddhist tradition where a monk is trying to escape the clutches of a hungry tiger. The monk finds himself at the edge of a cliff with the tiger directly behind him, and a stream filled with hungry crocodiles below. He says a silent prayer and leaps. On his way down he sees a bush on the side of the mountain and grabs it to break his fall. Soon after he catches his breath, two little gophers stick their heads out and begin gnawing on the bush. Serenely pondering his dilemma with the tiger above, the crocodiles below, and the gophers chewing away at his only support, he notices a luscious wild strawberry glistening with dew, just ready for picking. He reaches out, plucks the strawberry, and pops it in his mouth, and says smilingly, "How delicious; how delicious!"

We are emulating the mountain climber when we find ourselves holding on and trapped by our need for intellectual understanding and guarantees from the universe. The monk is free. He is not denying his plight; he simply chooses to focus on what is real in the present moment. Metaphorically, the mountain climber is the ego; the monk is the soul. Surrender is of the soul. The soul, our spiritual nature, already knows there is a God. The soul knows the Divine dwells within and help is always available.

I was not exposed to the spiritual concept of surrender when I was growing up. I learned about giving up and giving into the will of others, but I did not have a spiritual understanding or conscious experience of surrender. Giving up was a natural response to living in an alcoholic family. Because of my puny size and lack of athletic ability, giving up or going along with others were ways to survive. I also learned how to avoid looking like a victim by joking about my inabilities and shortcomings. I would give up, and feel like a victim, but I would not let it show.

I was a keen evaluator of my strengths and limitations. I would decide what I could accomplish, and what I could not, and simply choose the things I knew I would be good at. My belief in the power and love of God was overcome by my fear and insecurity, so I spent most of my time hanging on and feeling alone. If I was aware of the spiritual process of surrender, I did not allow myself to be conscious of it. It would have been much too frightening. I was too identified with my ego-consciousness. I was desperately clinging to this slender rope suspended over a precipice. If I let go I would die. That was an image of my life.

The notion of surrender in the material world means giving up. In the spiritual realm, surrender is not giving up, it is giving in. It is giving into and letting go to a power greater than the ego. We have all faced life situations when we have done all we can, including being open to all possible help, and yet the circumstance or situation still seems unsolvable. We have heard the advice: "Surrender; let go; detach; let go and let God." We might have heard these expressions over and again. Rarely, if ever, do we get an explanation or a direction of what we are supposed to do. What is this process of surrender? "Let Go and Let God; Surrender," we are told, but no one gives us any sense of how to accomplish this.

The struggle in "to let go or not let go" is one between the ego and the soul or our higher self, our spiritual nature. This conflict between holding on and letting go has been expressed in many ways: fear vs. love, the law of scarcity vs. the law of abundance, resistance vs. willingness, immediate gratification vs. long term growth, codependency vs. co-creation, and addiction/attachment vs. entering into the flow of life.

"What will happen if I let go?" we ask. "What will become of me if I surrender?" There are no definitive answers to those questions. It is understandable that we hold back because we are afraid. We do not know what is on the other side of surrender. We do not know what will happen to us if we "lose control" and let go. We ask, "What will I be like if I surrender?" "What will be left of the me I know now?"

When I identify solely with the ego, I am limited to this minute part of me that in both its fear and vanity tries to stand against the entire universe. So surely its method of defense is to hold on. My little ego is holding on for dear life. My poor little limited ego perceives change, transition, letting go, and transformation as death. My ego does not know if it will still exist on the other side of surrender. This is why there is so much struggling even to let go of something I need to let go of. Just imagine the mountain climber again. "Let go of the rope and you will be OK." "Really?" he asks. That is how frightened the little ego feels.

There have been many times in my life when I was struggling with an addiction or attachment, when I wanted to change, but I was fighting the process as well. I deeply desired change and yearned to let go. At the same time, I was deeply frightened of what was going to happen. Two often-quoted scriptures from Paul define this continuing challenge to release our identification with our ego-consciousness and to open ourselves to our Higher Being. "I do not do what I would like to do, but instead I do what I hate," (Ro 7:15) which is a grand description of life controlled by the ego, and "It is no longer I that live, but Christ who lives in me" (Ga 2:20) which is the height of spiritual consciousness.

For as long as it can, the ego holds onto all those things it considers important for its own survival. It holds onto control; it holds onto its own way of doing things; it holds onto the belief that it is right; it holds onto every defense in its attempt to remain safe and in control. It is usually only when each of us realizes how much pain our holding on is producing that letting go or surrender begins to become a possibility. Even then our ego and its primary partner, the thinking mind reenter the scene and attempt to convince us the situation is under control and everything is just as it should be. In other words, our limited, mortal nature tells us we really do not need to let go at all. The mind tells us to keep soldiering on and somehow we will be back in control again.

The ego cannot surrender. It is always holding on; it is taught to hold on; it thinks its survival is based on holding on. The only dimension where surrender can truly take place is within the Spirit, the Higher Self. It is the Spirit that must dominate for a moment for surrender to happen. In the moment of release, this instant of letting go, it is the Spirit that is in command, not the ego. We might say that as soon as we become willing to give our Spirit its power, the surrender or letting go begins to take place, even though we might not be aware of it yet. Letting go is the realization and the affirmation of a deeper, inner reality within us all.

Consider the classic example of Bill Wilson, one of the cofounders of Alcoholics Anonymous. After years of alcoholic drinking and the disasters it entailed, and many detoxifications, not knowing what he believed in, he cries out in despair, "If there be a God, let Him show Himself." This cannot be the ego talking. The ego by nature is always going to be looking for a way out. It is going to say something similar to, "Life is pretty gruesome right now, but as soon as we get over this one, everything will be OK." Then a little later, "Well, one drink won't hurt; you know you can handle one. What are you so worried about? You might not have been able to control it before but you've got a lot more sense now." The ego will go on and on with one rationalization after the other, attempting to stay in control. The ego is somewhat psychopathic in nature. It never learns from past mistakes. The ego practically invented the notion of insanity in "doing the same thing and expecting different results." When his soul cried out, Wilson discovered a power greater than the ego. He discovered a Higher Power. Surrender opens us to a connection with this Power, which many of us refer to as God.

We can only describe the process of surrender by going beyond the logic of the thinking mind. Surrender happens when the ego dies or winks out of existence for a moment and the Soul is the primary focus of our attention.

What is this space that a person experiences at the moment of surrender? It is called many things in different traditions: the cosmic void, the One, Unity Consciousness, becoming one with Spirit, the Kingdom of Heaven, nirvana, Samadhi, our own true nature. Surrender opens us to the place of Oneness, the place of deepest realization. In these moments of surrender and of unity consciousness, labels and distinctions are meaningless. All energies and forces become as one.

When the process of surrender and the power of our soul united with God takes over, we realize that what we had been holding onto all along is nothing and meaningless. We become aware that what we wanted to possess all along was something that we could never lose. In the eloquent words of the *A Course in Miracles*, we were "valuing that which is valueless," or we did not realize "nothing real can be threatened; nothing unreal exists." It is only in the letting go that we can open ourselves to these truths.

Surrender is the essence of all knowing; it brings us to the place where we stand, naked, face-to-face with ourselves, face-to-face with God, face-to-face with the universe, and face-to-face with one another. During the moment of surrender we might feel we are in a most terrifying place, and yet we can know it is also a place that is most sacred and holy. There is a beautifully haunting scene in *The Wind in the Willows*, when Rat and Mole come upon a sacred place where the god lives. They are overcome with awe in the Presence and Mole asks Rat if he is afraid. Rat replies, "Afraid! Afraid of Him? Oh, never, never! And yet—and yet—O Mole, I am afraid."

The beautiful paradox of surrender, of non-duality, is presented as an essential aspect of the spiritual path in all major forms of belief. The words of Jesus can serve as a continual reminder of the mystery of surrender: "Unless a grain of wheat fall into the earth and dies, it remains just a single grain; but if it dies, it bears much fruit." (Jn 12:24 NRSV)

There is an artistry to surrender. The brush must be held in gentle awareness.

OPENING TO SURRENDER

"LET GO? LET GO into what? *What will happen to me if I let go? Even if I wanted to let go I would not know how. I have been holding on for so long. Yes, I do want to let go. I am afraid, but I am even more tired than afraid. Oh, God…Is there a God? There must be; there has to be. I can no longer do what I have been doing. I can no longer hold on. I do not know what will happen when I let go or where it will take me. I could hold on a little longer, but I am not going to. I am letting go, now."*

Without surrender we would be continually trapped in a vision and mind-set limited by our ego's view of ourselves and the world. We would be what we are told we are; we would be what we thought everyone wanted us to be; we would only be the result of our education and our training. Like the baby eagle in the chicken's nest, we would never know we could fly. As little limited egos, we would always be seeking solace and comfort outside of ourselves. We would never experience happiness; we would never be living in the present, never experience moments of peace and harmony, because those moments are always later, or dependent on "if this happens" or "when that happens."

For much of my life, I never knew. I never had an inkling of who I really was. I was aware that fear was an unwanted but constant companion, and I spent much of my time constructing a mask of self-assurance. As I reflect on my past, I see clearly that I molded my persona according to the people I was with at particular times. At home I was the quiet, lost/hero-child desperately wanting and needing affirmation but seldom getting what I was seeking. I am not blaming anyone; I was either afraid to ask for what I needed or I did not know how to ask. In school I was the show-off, the class clown. My yin and yang were always at odds with one another. One side was always looking for the hook to get some attention, and another side was painfully shy and horribly frightened at what I thought other people were thinking about me. I knew I had a soul and a spiritual nature, but it never had any power. It never did anything. My soul just sort of sat there, while the rest of me was scrambling around trying to make sense of life. Without my knowing it, everyone and everything around me fed my continuing identification with my limited little ego-consciousness. I was so incredibly lost thinking I was only a struggling ego in the midst of overpowering obstacles.

The process of surrender creates a state of awareness or awakening that transforms how we see ourselves, how we perceive others, and how we respond to the world around us. There are many circumstances that can begin to open our awareness. The events can be as dramatic as an illness or divorce, but drama and magnitude are not necessary aspects of waking up. Awakening to our true nature could be triggered by something as simple as a sunset, the laughter of a child, a look, or a touch. Even a memory can begin to bring us to a deeper self-awareness. For most of us the awakening to our spiritual nature is more gradual rather than sudden. We have a vague hunger, a foggy recollection, an obscure longing for something more than we are presently experiencing.

With only this faint idea and fleeting glimpse of our spiritual self, it is only natural that we would become more and more involved and identified with the outside world. Before we are more fully awake and aware, we continue to think we are these little egos in this great big universe, feeling overwhelmed and incomplete and searching for someone or something to make us feel strong, capable, and whole. Because of the ego's uncertainty about itself and its abilities, it is only natural that we would begin our search for the completion and wholeness we crave outside of ourselves. There are more than a few things out there which will get our attention: food, money, sex, alcohol, drugs, success, and status. The list is close to endless. All of these things offer us the promise of wholeness, but we find out to our dismay that the promise was an illusion.

When I look back at myself as that scared, insecure little kid, I realize I was just looking for a way to function in the world and to be as content and free as possible. When I broke away from home, the outside world became *Alice In Wonderland.* "Eat me, drink me, try me," so many things seemed to be saying. All those outside things carried with them the hidden promise, "I will make you whole and happy."

My first fix was food. I loved to eat, and my mother was a great cook, but I was always skinny and runty and since I ran track all through my high school years, I never put on any weight. After high school, I entered a Roman Catholic religious order and went far away from home for my training. At the novitiate I began to eat and eat. It was a complicated addiction. Being stuffed made me feel good, or at least stopped me from feeling bad. I also found that since I had a tremendous capacity for food, far beyond my size, I could get a lot of attention for the huge quantities I could consume. With all of that going on I quickly ballooned from 115 to 165 pounds. I am short and small-boned so even 5 or 10 pounds stands out on me. Food was an addiction that really showed on me, while many other addictions are more subtle and hidden.

For many of us who realize our journey on earth is a spiritual one, there comes an event or series of events which push us to a point of letting go or surrender. It might be an addiction that pushes us to hit bottom. It might be the inexplicable loss of a loved one; the event might take the form of some other crisis in our lives; it might be a time when we become disappointed and disillusioned, when whatever it was that we were holding onto was no longer working; or perhaps a moment when we were at the end of our logical rope, when no explanation was satisfying. It is with any of those experiences, including such simpler ones as the birth of a child, or the wonder at the beauty of a flower, that we can be pushed to the point of surrender. Whatever vehicle might take us to this moment, we become consciously aware there is nothing that we can do to change what is happening in our lives. It is this deep realization of helplessness that can open the door to the Spirit and a deeper understanding of the Self.

Surrender is the process which opens us up to the inner reality of our spiritual nature. It allows us to see an aspect of ourselves which has hidden behind the facades of the material world. In this act of surrender, two seemingly different parts of ourselves come together. It is a rejoining of our ego and our Spirit. Surrender creates an integration of these two aspects of ourselves which have been separate and at odds for so long. This open door of surrender and the inner realizations it brings are at the heart of the spiritual process. The chain of events leading up to surrender, along with the results of the process, is sometimes referred to as a "spiritual awakening." That is a marvelous description, because surrender truly results in an awakening to the Spirit. It is not just an awakening to our individual spiritual strength and wholeness, but to the vast realm of Grace that encompasses all beings. This soul of ours, our spiritual nature, is our link to a higher power and a connection with the Spirit and soul of every other being as well. It is at this moment of surrender and letting go, that we can realize that we are more than this little ego. We become "soul conscious." We get a sense of our spiritual self, this part of us that is expansive, unconditionally loving, and gracious without end.

We probably had a faint notion that something much greater than our limited sense of ego existed within us, but we never let ourselves be sure. Paul put it beautifully when he said that now we "see like a dim image in a mirror." (1 Co 13:12) Surrender is like turning on the light; we realize that we had been in the dark and sleeping all of this time, and what we thought was a dream, or this vague notion of God and Self, was reality instead. Looking through the eyes of the Spirit we will see ourselves, the world, others, and God in very different ways than we would if we were looking through the eyes of the ego.

Surrender does not happen on a conscious level. It happens deeply within the individual, and cannot take place by pushing or brute force. Because surrender is such an interior process, there can be no absolute directives in this area. No one can tell you how to surrender. You can learn, however, to do all the necessary work to get to the point of release. As with grieving, it is more that you allow the process to happen, rather than doing anything in an overtly active way. You become a willing participant as this process, this deep spiritual movement, takes place within you. Your active involvement is more of a stepping out of the way; it is more of an acceptance of the process and allowing it to happen. One of many paradoxes in this mystery is, "In order to surrender, I must first surrender."

A few years ago during some therapeutic work, I had a real breakthrough session. I was energized and excited; I remember thanking my therapist effusively. He looked at me lovingly, smiled, and said, "All I had to do was get out of your way." Surrender is getting out of my own way, and lovingly, yet powerfully, letting the process of grace and Spirit happen.

Of course, there is not just one big surrender in life and then we arrive. Surrender requires a continual conscious effort to keep the door open, and with that effort, the realization that life and growth are an ongoing process of surrender. Each time we surrender, each time we let go, we open ourselves to greater awareness of our spiritual nature. As long as we are alive and willing to follow the path of Spirit, we will be surrendering. Also, each time we experience this process of surrender our egos can become a little more docile, a little more manageable, and a little more in their proper place. It is easy when we begin to touch our spiritual nature and begin to get a more authentic picture of who we are to want to deny our ego-self, or to try to bash it into submission. As with all aspects of life, one of the keys here is balance. The work of the spiritual path is not to destroy or eliminate the ego. We simply become more aware that the ego is not who we are. We are always encouraged to embrace our humanity, which is this integral combination of ego and Spirit.

Surrender is truly the reunion of seemingly diverse parts of the self. It is a reunion of the ego and the Spirit, both of which have a voice of their own. Surrender is not essentially a process of giving up but one of giving in. It is a giving in to a larger, more encompassing part of self. It is opening to the Spirit and Higher Consciousness. It is important to note the only thing that is given up is the seeming supremacy of the ego. The ego is neither lost nor destroyed, simply relegated to its proper place and function.

Although there are many roads to surrender, there are three aspects that stand out more than others: love, awareness, and acceptance.

The process of surrender is a process of love. It is surrender into the Beloved, into the One. It is a letting go of the ego, that part of us that does not know love. True loving is volitional surrender, not of who we are, but a letting go of those barriers or defenses that prevent honest and wholehearted disclosure and discovery. The beloved could be Self, God, or another person; in a deep sense these are all identical. In this loving state, dualities have less and less substance until they finally become meaningless. This perhaps is the supreme surrender, the realization that it is no longer necessary to make separations or comparisons.

Surrender becomes possible in the state of loving awareness, and awareness itself is a key to the process of surrender. If we let ourselves become fully aware of what we are doing, whether it is smoking, eating too much, any addictive behavior, anything that is harmful, or habits that we no longer want, these things will drop off from us like an old cloak for which we no longer have use. Imagine what it would be like to allow ourselves to be completely aware, for a full twenty-four hours, of just one habitual behavior we would like to release. We would be easily purified before the year was over. Yet we know from experience the ego distracts us with all its petty and sometimes totally unnecessary demands. While we cater to the ego aspect of self, awareness of the true self diminishes and our holding on intensifies.

We cannot become aware through the ego, for its time frame is always the past and the future. The ego cannot be in the present moment, so it can never truly be aware. If awareness is one of the keys to surrender, then surrender must be now, in this moment.

Acceptance is powerful, but it does not have to be a conflict. As soon as we hold surrender as a fight or a struggle, we have let the ego back into control. The ego loves a fight, and once the fight begins the ego is off and running. It is so easy to want to fight with distracting or disturbing thoughts, to crush them, to argue with them, to beat them to death, and yet as soon as we get sucked into this process we have allowed the ego to be in charge again.

Here is another paradox; surrender involves no struggle at all. Every winter our home is invaded by a host of little orange lady bugs. They seem to congregate mostly in the kitchen. Now, it is not as if they are all over everything. Usually there are only about five or six of them visible at a time, but I still find them annoying. I have searched for solutions, but have not been satisfied with any of them. A friend of mine, noting my frustration, suggested, "How about just loving them." As ridiculous as that sounded, I begrudgingly agreed it might be the only solution.

A few months ago we were talking to our little granddaughter, Aoife, and somehow the subject of lady bugs came up, and I told her about all the lady bugs in our kitchen. She immediately piped up and said, "Bring me some!"

I do not know if I have loved the lady bugs as much as I could, but I do know now, whenever I see them, instead of just being annoyed, I hear a sweet little voice saying, "Bring me some."

Notice how we balk at letting go of something we think we should be able to control. The how-about-just-loving-them solution is a powerful reminder that surrender might have little to do with changing external situations. It might have everything to do with how we look at things.

In working with a client the other day, she pictured her ego as a crying little baby and her Higher Self as a loving old Father Time figure, smiling and laughing. After doing some integrating work she said, "You know, that little baby was just doing what it was doing because it was all it knew how to do. It only knew how to scream and squawk and yell and try to control. It was operating out of fear, and once it realized it was not alone, it became much more manageable." No struggle, just love, awareness, and acceptance.

If it is true that at the moment of surrender I recognize this spiritual and more real side of myself, then the converse is also true, when I am not in conscious contact with this spiritual side of myself then I am controlled by my ego-consciousness which in turn is influenced by all my addictions, attachments, and codependency needs. It is sometimes discouraging for me to think of this, for when I look at a day in my life, and the moments of that day, I find I am much more in the consciousness of scarcity and addiction than in the consciousness of abundance, freedom, and non-duality.

In exploring some of the many ways that surrender or letting go takes place in our lives, we can come to a deeper inner realization of the process and mystery of surrender, this miraculous process that continually opens us up to a greater, larger, more loving reality.

As we continue to develop a deeper respect and understanding of surrender and all the varied ways that it shows in our everyday life, all of us might be able to allow this process of deep inner awakening to occur more easily, readily, and lovingly. The process of surrender can manifest very simply; it does not have to be expressed in dramatic ways. The process can be as simple as letting go of a value that is not our own, or listening to our own inner voice leading us in a direction of the heart. In listening to that voice we might find ourselves loving ourself where we are at this moment rather than focusing on the ego work of people pleasing.

This is a journey, a journey into our life, and our own inner being. It is a journey of discovery; a journey of awakening; a journey of surrender.

INTRODUCTION TO MEDITATION

• Create a comfortable time and place for this exercise. It is best to create time and space when you will not be disturbed. Know that if your attention is needed for another situation that you will immediately return to full waking consciousness. As you get comfortable, relaxed, and open, take a few deep, cleansing breaths, opening even more.

• Count backwards from ten to one with each lowering number experiencing yourself more and more open, more and more relaxed. You can even imagine you are on an elevator or escalator moving from the tenth floor to the first. Now, as you pass through each floor you become more and more open, more and more relaxed. You do not sleep; you feel a sense of lightness and receptiveness as you allow Spirit to speak to you, sharing with you exactly what you need.

• Let the positive energies of love, light, and healing begin to resonate in your consciousness.

• Gently now, moving from the tenth floor to the ninth, let your breathing deepen naturally. Nothing is forced.

• From the ninth floor to the eighth and the seventh, you are becoming more open and more relaxed. Becoming more and more relaxed, open to grace, to the inner wisdom of God that dwells within you.

• From the seventh floor through the sixth and fifth, you are becoming more and more relaxed.

• From the fifth floor to the fourth and third, more and more relaxed, more and more open.

• From the third to the second to the first you are becoming more and more relaxed and open.

• And as you get off the elevator or escalator, you find a comfortable space and a place to sit or recline.

MEDITATION: SURRENDER

Breathe deeply now and let go. Imagine you
are just floating. You are weightless. Just
enjoy that for a moment. Breathe. Breathe
deeply now and just float for awhile.

Pause...

As you are floating you hear a sound. It is a telephone ringing. You pick
it up and a voice speaks to you about something you are concerned
with.

Before you begin to generate too much concern, notice how that fear or
worry has pulled you out of that marvelous state of floating and being
free.

Nothing has changed, except now your mind is clinging to something.
That something was there a moment ago, but you were not thinking
about it, you were not giving it any energy. A moment ago you were free.
Now you are not.

Let go of any anger or annoyance, just become gently aware of how
powerful and restricting your thoughts can be. Notice the difference
between being free of attachment, when you were floating, and now.
No blame or shame, just become aware.

Know that you now have more of a choice. When thoughts intrude on
your sense of peace, acknowledge them, and let them go. You are much
more than that.

Pause...

Thank yourself for this lesson.

Pause...

You will learn more and more of how to be free as you progress.

CLOSING FOR MEDITATION

Begin to be conscious again of your breathing. Feel yourself in your body. Breathe deeply as you come fully back.

Breathe deeply and stretch. Come fully back here in your body, completely centered and grounded.

Get up, stretch, and look around you. Become familiar with the place again, feeling yourself in your body.

You might choose to take a few moments to either sit with the experience or journal about it, or you might wait until later to process the meditation.

NUGGETS

Surrender only happens when we are ready. We cannot make surrender happen, but we can contribute to our readiness.

Buddha suggested all suffering comes from attachment. How does that fit for you?

What would it be like to be free?

Who are you without your stuff?

What happens when you let go of the rope?

Have you ever had a "how delicious" moment?

The ego is not evil; it is just three years old. Did you ever try to argue with a three year old? Did you notice how quickly you got sucked in? Did you notice the only way you won was because you were bigger or because you fell back on "Because I said so"?

AWARENESS

I AM SO OBLIVIOUS *sometimes. Not on purpose, I'm just wrapped up in my own little world. I have a job, concern, fear, or worry and it consumes me. My world contracts around that attachment and it is all that I see. It is all I am interested in. Then something happens to open the doorways of my consciousness, and I see that the world is not just made up of my limited little zones of black and white. The world is a glorious rainbow of color, a huge spectrum of emotion, and this whole panorama was available to me, but I was an ego looking down instead of a soul looking up and out.*

Surrender and awareness are parallel tracks on the spiritual path. The more we become aware, the more we surrender. The more we surrender, the more we become aware.

There is a deep core awareness within us that continually moves us towards the truth. Initially this movement might show itself as vague dissatisfaction with life or present itself in the form of a more overt question such as, "Is that all there is?"

It is a mystery why some people choose to dive deeper into life while others seem to be content to skim the surface. The grace of restlessness and dissatisfaction with the material world is in all of us. For some the exploration will lead to existential despair; for others, sainthood.

The awareness which produces spiritual understanding goes beyond the qualities of the intellect. Spiritual concepts by their nature extend beyond the grasp of the thinking mind. In surrender, we are stretching ourselves beyond the intellect. Although there are many seeming contradictions that arise in exploring surrender, we can discover we have the capacity to go beyond the limited view of the intellect without that much of a struggle.

Before I can make my life a process of continual surrender, I have to be awake; I have to be aware. I am reminded of what the mystic Gurdjief said, "You have to realize you are in prison before you can get out." That line always cracks me up because it is so simple and so true. Part of me has to be out of the box, not trapped, in order for me to realize the rest of me is trapped!

Along with promoting the ability to recognize the situation I am experiencing, awareness is also the realization that I do not have to be totally identified with the situation. It is only then that I can act in a positive way. It was Einstein who said, "The significant problems we have cannot be solved at the same level of thinking with which we created them." He gives us a wonderful description of what spiritual teachers refer to as the inner witness or the Observer consciousness.

We all possess this internal gift; we all have this wise and compassionate consciousness within us called the Observer or the Witness.

The Observer Self is a spiritual quality through which I become aware. Through that awareness, I open myself to the Power of Spirit through surrender.

Imagine what it would be like to have the most positive, loving, and wise therapist always available to you. Whenever you had a difficulty or even a question, this entity would immediately enter your consciousness. No matter what your obstacle, there would be no judgment or blaming, only loving presence, compassion, and understanding.

We all possess this internal gift; we all have this wise and compassionate consciousness within us called the Observer or the Witness. It is a quality of our spiritual nature where we experience a Zen-like sense of detachment. In this realm we continue to feel and experience whatever a situation might be producing in us, but we are not overwhelmed or excessively identified with it.

The Observer might view a difficult day this way:

"I'm really having a rotten day. I wish I wasn't, but here I am. I know some things that have contributed to this. I noticed a scrape on my car this morning that must have happened in the parking lot yesterday. That really annoys me and brings me down. I have been taking such good care of this car."

"I was so annoyed this morning I let that feeling control me, I was abrupt and rude to my wife. I know she understands my moodiness, but I need to make amends."

"I didn't exercise this morning, and I know that contributes to my negativity. I need to make sure I budget time for that and get up early enough."

"I am going to ask forgiveness of anyone I might have hurt or disturbed during this episode of un-awareness. I will work on being more aware of the things that pull me off center. I also choose to be grateful for being aware now, and for being open to the present grace of growth and transformation."

Notice how the internal dialogue with the Observer Self creates awareness rather than blame. It also offers solutions rather than guilt. The Observer uses awareness as a way of avoiding similar negative situations in the future as well. Feelings are neither denied nor made the measure of things.

The Observer is a built-in "instant replay" mechanism. Unlike the ego, which would use many life incidents to increase blame, shame, and guilt, the soul uses the power of the Observer to create positive, healthy, and long-lasting solutions. My awareness allows me to step out of a particular situation, so I am not overwhelmed by it nor overly identified with it. From this place of the Observer or witness, I can see a much larger picture, and be aware of the many alternatives for action rather than experiencing myself as being stuck or trapped.

The Observer should not be confused with the psychological defense mechanism of disassociation. In disassociation, the person is disconnected from the experience. He experiences it as if it is happening to someone else, and most emotions are either covered up or denied. The Observer aspect of our soul is not separate from the experience nor does it block the feelings and emotions that are occurring. More than anything else, the Observer helps us realize we are much more than what we are experiencing.

The gift of awareness is also a reminder that surrender is not simply a passive act. This quality of awareness is an essential element for many, if not all, of the foundations of spiritual living such as being in the present moment, opening to the Observer consciousness, practicing of the presence of God, positive choice making, and of course, surrendering. Without awareness none of these actions is possible.

There have been many times when I have reviewed a day or a week in my life and have realized I was not present at all. I was sleepwalking. Where was I? I know I went to work. I know I had a cup of coffee. I know I did this job and that job, but was I really present?

During how much of a day are we really aware? Do our days just simply run into each other? Examine the Thank-God-It's-Friday syndrome. We find ourselves so looking forward to the weekend and concentrating on getting off work that we are not really *at* work. We are so looking forward to the weekend that anything coming up during the week is a distraction or an annoyance. Nearly everything is a constant reminder that we are *not* at the weekend, and of course every moment I am thinking about the weekend, I am not aware of the present.

It is easy, too easy, terribly easy, to go through part of a day, a whole day and even longer, perhaps a lifetime, without being aware. Unawareness makes us continual victims of the "slings and arrows of outrageous fortune." When we are sleep walking, we are not living life, and we do not even realize that we are oblivious to life's wonders.

In the movie *The Sand Pebbles*, Steve McQueen is dying in a forsaken village in China, and with his last breath he screams to no one in particular, "I was home, what happened?" How many stories have we heard of someone waking up one morning and wondering who they are and where they are going? We can call it anything from midlife crisis to job dissatisfaction, but suddenly a reality that we had not known was there hits us right in the face.

One reason I enjoy working with other people is that I have to be present to them. I have to be right there, listening and aware, and I really have to focus on being present. I know my clients could sense if I were there with them, or if I were thinking about lunch or my furnace or my bank account balance. Not many people would come back to a therapist who was not present.

Admittedly, there are certain comforts that come from a predictable routine, but when the routine robs us of consciousness, we pay the price of living unconsciously and taking our lives for granted. We become so acclimated to the circumstances of our lives, and we miss so much. The somnambulant drone of the commonplace can put us in a daze and hinder us from experiencing a sense of gratitude and wonder as we sleepwalk through life.

Almost effortlessly, most of us simply become acclimated and desensitized to everything in the world around us. The people and circumstances in our lives become all too familiar. Our senses will easily filter out what we think or perceive is unnecessary information, and in this process of self-absorption and unawareness, our lives become contracted into a tiny, painful, and cramped world view. We are oblivious to many wonderful and beautiful life experiences. If we happen to be in survival mode, we will not stop to smell the roses; we will not even see them. If we are wrapped up in our own stuff, either consciously or unconsciously, then anybody else's stuff including our spouse's or our children's will just seem unimportant to us. Asleep in our own little world, we will not be aware of anyone's concerns except our own.

When I am in this prison of self-absorption, it would be absolutely amazing to me if someone were to point out that I was being selfish and self-centered. How could I possibly know I was being self-centered or selfish? I was simply doing what I was doing. I was doing what came naturally. When accused of not really listening by someone, I might be shocked. It was not a conscious choice on my part. I was only aware of a fragment of reality, but I was not aware that this was only a limited segment. To me, in this state of mind, I am like a person with blinders on who does not know they have blinders on.

There are numerous reasons I might not want to be aware or why I might choose unawareness. The first is that reality has a painful side. If I want to be up, happy, and joyful all the time, then I will need to cover up the other emotional experiences that life inevitably brings such as sorrow, sadness, hurt, fear, and loneliness.

We might choose to be unaware of these things, or we might choose to block their intensity either through denial or some other means. Unless we are willing to be open and accepting of who we are and what we are experiencing at this moment, we will find all sorts of ways to cultivate unawareness.

When I "wake up" I often wonder how much of my life has been spent sleep walking. When I become aware of the sweetness of my grandkids or look at my wife and realize how much I love her or just simply become aware of the comfort and nurturing I get from a hot shower in the morning, I am amazed at the gift of awareness. From awareness flows gratitude, the present moment, and connection to God and the universe.

Introvert that I am, I am usually quite protective of my space, but there have been many times in a grocery line, bookstore, or airport when I have chosen to interact with other people and been blessed with a smile, a sense of harmony, beauty, and Oneness. How many of those moments have I missed because I have been wrapped up in my own limited awareness?

Even if we have allowed ourselves to be awake and aware, the ego will continue to be fearful of greater awareness. Our present awareness has become comfortable to us, even though we might realize it is limited. We know that by opening the doors of our awareness we will push ourselves towards change, possible risks, and unknown territory. With this sense of change and challenge comes the ego's fear of death and annihilation.

The ego's fears can become quite cunning and subtle. Perhaps we really do want to change, but we are afraid of doing it wrong or not knowing how. We are afraid of what might be asked of us. Therefore, we block our awareness, and hold to the notion that if we remain unaware then we won't have to face the fear and risk changing. Although this defense is much like an ostrich sticking its head in the sand, the ego still likes to think, "If I don't acknowledge it's there, then maybe it isn't."

The incidents which trigger fear and produce this constricted view of ourselves and the world can happen almost anywhere and at any time. These events could be something as simple as a loud noise or an angry voice, and often they are not even really threatening in themselves, but our minds have made them so. Many times these fear reactions are associated with feelings of shame and inadequacy that we learned when we were young. When we are in this limited frightened state of consciousness it is so easy to constrict. Someone or something comes along and triggers this self-protective response and our awareness becomes even less than before. Our scope of vision becomes contracted. Our view of ourselves and the world is contracted into this tiny little box that we mistakenly call reality.

Our limited awareness contracts us into what we think of as a safe place. When our primitive protective instincts come on line, all our energies are pulled in. We become like a fortress with the draw-bridge up, all gates secured, and the archers at the turrets ready for action. All that focus on protection negates any awareness of the beauty of the sky or the warm touch of the wind. We might not even be too concerned if one of our loved ones wanted to carry on a conversation. Rather than having empathy for another, we would be morbidly interested in our own safety and protection. The unfortunate thing is that most of us live in that constricted place. We are on constant red or yellow alert, and we are not even aware of our limited scope of vision. This constriction and contraction is one of the many vicious circles that can keep us trapped in an unaware life. We stay where we are because we have learned to be afraid to move, and we remain afraid to move because where we are is at least familiar. All of these reactions can occur below the conscious mind. We might know or intuit something is wrong, but because of the strength of our fear and discomfort that sense of wrongness gets projected onto other people, places, and things. We might even convince ourselves that we are justified in feeling the way we do and wonder what is wrong with the rest of the world. Paradoxically, the tighter the constriction the more likely we are to feel it and wake up!

Awareness is a deep spiritual challenge. It means, first and foremost, looking at ourselves honestly and completely. It means being responsible for our thoughts, feelings, and actions. It means living in the present, and living in the practice of being free from fear and guilt. It means looking at our shadow side, all those things we have been taught are unacceptable. It means having ears that hear and eyes that see. "He that has ears let him hear." (Mt 11:15) Life can become much fuller for us by increased awareness. We will move from a stance of unhealthy self-centeredness to the realization that we are children of the universe and have a role and responsibility to play in the growth and restoration of this planet.

During one of my psychology courses, years ago, I was asked to walk along the street and focus on just being aware of one specific color or shape. I would spend some time just looking for the color orange, then looking for ovals, and then looking for purple. To this day it is amazing to me how much more I saw and became aware of. It wasn't that I did not see these things before; it was just that they did not register. I was programmed to just see what was necessary such as not bumping into people or watching the traffic. Meanwhile there was a whole world of purple, orange, ovals, and squares that I was missing. There is a whole world filled with beauty, children of God, love, heartache, joy, tears, and more.

I miss so much of the world when I am asleep or unaware.

Although the senses and the intellect may be the gateway for our learning and perception, it is a deeper aspect of self that brings true awareness. It is only beyond the mind that these deep inner realms are reached. We use the mind to stretch as far as it can go, then we must leap beyond the intellect, perhaps even with some fear, but always experiencing a yearning and awareness there is something beyond and deeper than our thinking mind.

So often my own thinking is black and white. I find myself approaching life situations with the sense that there are only two solutions to a problem, or only two choices, one white and one black. I am usually not happy with either one. Then someone comes along and points out other choices that can be made and a whole new world is open to me that I had never realized existed. That is absolutely amazing to me. When that new awareness opens to me, it is almost as if I am given a new faculty or ability. Perhaps that is a good way of looking at awareness or the process of becoming aware. It is like putting on a new pair of glasses.

Outside of San Francisco is a beautiful setting filled with redwoods and sequoias. John Muir Park has the feel of a sacred, outdoor cathedral. Once when Margo and I were there we only had a limited time to explore. There were two hiking trails. One took an hour to complete and the other fifteen minutes; we had forty-five minutes. One was too long and we would never make it back on time, and the other was so short it didn't seem worth it. I became terribly agitated and conflicted; we only had two choices and both of them were rotten. Margo, as usual, saw things differently. She said, "We will take the long trail and walk down for twenty minutes then turn around and walk back."

I was stunned. She broke the rules! In my old way of thinking you only have two choices, the long trail or the short one, nothing in between. It was amazing to me there were other possibilities. My mind became exuberantly free, and I began to play with all the possibilities I had not thought of previously. "We could walk the short path three times. We could walk the short path twice and then spend fifteen minutes on the long trail." The possibilities were endless! Whenever I get the opportunity I ask one of our granddaughters, "What does Goldilocks say?" She responds with an impish smile, "It's just right!" How beautiful. It's not too hot or too cold, not too big or too small, not too hard or too soft, it's just right. Goldilocks would have been a pretty unhappy girl if she was only aware of the extremes of life. She searched beyond the extremes to find something better. How often do I get stuck in just thinking there is only one way to do things or only one possible outcome?

Awareness is more than simply knowing something. There is an obvious difference between knowing and awareness. A few years ago, many people realized corporations were dumping toxic waste where it would be harmful. Perhaps many realized that our resources are finite, but the facts did not even begin to change the reality. It is awareness that begins to foster change. There is a subtle but powerful dynamic that exists when consciousness becomes aware instead of simply knowing. Awareness is the beginning of change–in here lies its ultimate importance. When we become aware, we can never really become unaware again. The energies of awareness slowly move us towards change and growth.

There is also a shadow side to this wonderful gift and energy of awareness. As with any other power, it can be misused. Genuine and complete awareness leads to a deeper understanding and acceptance of self and others, but even as we open to the gift of awareness, we will probably experience it in an incomplete and limited way. A limited awareness can lead to terrible self-judgment. We are encouraged to use this newfound awareness to create positive change rather than negative self-punishment. Rather than limiting us, we want to allow our awareness to let us see what we could not see before, and expand our choices and actions.

Even when we take the risk of being aware, and open ourselves to awareness, there are some difficulties. For some of us, even amid deep and spectacular awareness, we can choose to focus on the negative side of things. We can focus on the side of scarcity rather than that of abundance. We can focus on fear rather than love.

We are still growing. Although we are moving towards perfection, we are not there yet. We are attempting to do the best we can with what we understand or are aware of at the moment. After taking a particular course of action we might become aware of a whole other set of circumstances, ideas, or choices we could have made. We need to use this learning to do things differently–not to beat ourselves up for something we were not aware of before.

There is an important distinction to make between guilt and awareness. Guilt is the attitude or action of self-punishment, which gets us nowhere. When we speak of guilt, in a positive way, we are referring to a feeling or a sense which can prevent us from making a similar misstep again. So often, though, guilt becomes a form of self-punishment and does not prevent similar mistakes. That inner sense which promotes positive action would be better called awareness rather than guilt.

One of the most powerful gifts of awareness is that it is also the key that unlocks the door or doors of our addictions. Awareness banishes denial. It is the open door to change. Once we are aware of a negative or self-destructive behavior, it is much more difficult for us to keep doing it. Awareness is not simply knowing with the mind; it is knowing with all of our being. We can know that smoking is not healthy for us, and the only difference that knowing will make for us is that it will add to the guilt and shame we already feel. It does not change the behavior. When we know a truth in our bones, however, that is when change begins to happen.

I know I need to cultivate this Observer consciousness. When I am identified with my ego-consciousness, I am only aware of my ego and its needs. Other people and their needs are just in my way. It is when I am connected to my soul and the Infinite that I can step back from my ego and its needs. I can also have some distance from my emotions and even the thoughts of my intellect. As I step back I begin to discover I am more than my thoughts, my feelings, and my ego. I might not have a clear sense of who I am yet, but I know what I am not. There is a much larger me waiting to be discovered.

MEDITATION: AWARENESS

As you get comfortable, relaxed, and open,
take a few deep cleansing breaths, opening
even more.

Count backwards from ten to one as you
breathe deeply. You can feel a sense of lightness and receptiveness as
you allow Spirit to speak to you, sharing with you exactly what you need.

Imagine now you are a satellite in space. You have all sorts of antennas
projecting outward. You are picking up all sorts of information, sights,
sounds, radio and TV signals, cell phone calls, and text messages from
millions of people.

Concentrate on sound for a moment. Focus on a larger city below you.
Stretch your hearing sense down to that city and begin to listen to all the
sounds that are happening there. Notice all the many things you can
hear: traffic, air hammers, honking, voices, angry voices, sad voices,
happy voices, noises of cooking, cleaning, and all other sorts of sounds.

Pause...

Now imagine you are receiving visual input from the city. Begin to be
aware of all the images that are coming to you: people, buildings,
machinery, trees, flowers, kids, grownups. What do you see? What are
you drawn to?

Pause...

All this is always going on around you; all this and more.

How little we are aware of most of the time.

Pause...

Now, imagine yourself walking down a street in your neighborhood and looking around. What would it be like to walk down that street for the first time? Let go of opinion or any other judgmental voices; your job right now is to be aware. As you are aware of your home for the first time, what catches your attention? What pulls at the focus of your awareness? Is it something that is really important to you; is it something you value; or do you find yourself putting importance on what someone else might think is important?

This is just an example of being open to awareness.

Be open to expanding your awareness and consciousness today.

How can you do that? Will you look more, listen more? What will you do today to expand your awareness?

How do you experience your expanded awareness? How can it affect your life and your relationship with others?

Breathe.

Begin to be conscious again of your breathing. Breathe deeply and stretch. Come fully back here in your body, completely centered and grounded.

Get up, stretch, and look around you. Become familiar with the place again, feeling yourself in your body. Journal or process any other way you like.

NUGGETS

"Me, me, me, I, I, I," that is the self-centered world of unawareness. Notice how painful it is.

Be careful. Your ego's limited perception can use awareness as a beat-yourself-up guilt machine.

The lead character in a movie called *Skin Deep* cries, "I've got it! You can't stop a problem until you realize what it is, but you can't realize what it is until you stop doing it."

In the awareness which goes beyond rational explanation, God can be both personal and indefinable.

Surrender has allowed me to go beyond the limited consciousness of my ego. I realize now that I was attempting to address my inner hunger and emptiness through my addictions. I now approach those hungers and needs through my soul, the way they needed to be addressed in the first place.

There is also much awareness that takes place internally, but it is only in the quiet of our hearts that we get in touch with this deeper reality.

When I look at what I did in the past through the lens of today's understanding, many times I see that I have fallen short. Awareness is not about blame; awareness is about learning and transformation.

Keep in mind that blame, shame, and guilt are the ego's way of attempting change.

Another term for awareness is *perception* or perhaps a better way of putting it: awareness is the broadest possible perception.

A limited sense of awareness can lead us to identifying with the problem or the situation. More of a total awareness leads us to be outside the box, to recognize the situation, but not to be identified with it.

What would it be like if I were continually aware that I am loved?

I WILL NOT LET YOU GO
UNTIL YOU BLESS ME

"WHAT'S THE LESSON HERE?" My friend Molly asked that question over and over as she repeatedly paced back and forth in her living room. "What's the lesson here?"

We are often told, "Everything is a blessing." It does not always feel that way. In difficult life circumstances, the blessing is sometimes not easy to recognize. Perhaps a more practical way to approach life is by knowing, "Everything is a learning or a challenge to grow."

Before I met Molly I do not think I ever looked at life as a learning experience or a set of lessons. I was just hanging out, being knocked around by life and trying to manage as best as I could. Sometimes I could work out an explanation about what was happening to me, and at other times I would fall victim to circumstances that did not seem to have any meaning for me at all. Then, one evening years ago, I was with my friend Molly, and she was having a difficult time. I listened to her and was as supportive as I knew how to be. Suddenly, she sprang up from her chair and started pacing, saying out loud with all the anger and earnestness she could muster, "What's the lesson here?" It was a plea and a prayer. "What's the lesson here?" "What am I supposed to be learning?" The prayer closed with, "Help me to learn whatever it is I need to learn, so I can get out of this box; so I can get out of this pain and confusion." What a beautiful piece of wisdom I received that night. "What's the lesson here?" I come back to that question often. It is not a question about cosmic causality. It is not a question reflective of self-pity such as "Why did this happen to me?" No, it is a deeply personal and spiritual question: "What is it right here, in this situation, that I need to learn?" "How can I grow from this?" "How can I become more loving, kinder, more at peace in handling this?"

One of my favorite Old Testament stories is that of Jacob and the angel. In the story, Jacob gets into a wrestling match with this stranger. I am not certain as to what started it all, but they wrestled all night long and went at it so strenuously that Jacob's hip was knocked out. As the sun began to rise, the angel finally said, "Let me go," and Jacob, realizing by this time that he is struggling with a supernatural being, says, "No, you're not going yet...I will not let you go until you bless me." "I will not let you go until you bless me." (Gn 32:26 NRSV) I love that line.

"I will not let you go until you bless me" is not always my usual way of operating. If something is bothering me, or getting in my way, my tendency is to get even angrier and annoyed and want to get rid of this thing that is so troubling. The "throw away" method, or suppression and repression as it is called in psychology, does not work. These defenses are not really solutions, they are simply ways of sweeping the dirt under the carpet or tossing a blanket over the elephant in the living room. When I pretend something is not there or try to push it out of my mind, I am simply covering it up. I am not taking care of it. Denial or repression would be like putting makeup over my measles spots. I am attempting to hide the symptoms without addressing or even admitting to the real problem. Pretending-it's-not-there or if-I-ignore-it-it-will-go-away are defenses that have been with me most of my life. I am always amazed at how often I use them even though I know from experience they do not work. Magical thinking grabs me sometimes and hints, "Well, maybe it will work this time."

Eventually, if we stay aware, we recognize the "throw away" method is ineffective and unproductive. We begin to realize that using either brute force or denial to deal with life, only gives our difficulties more energy. For example, if we are trying to meditate and distractions come along, which they will inevitably do, the tendency is to get into a fight with them, and to try to push them away. We become angry at these distracting thoughts because they are keeping us from the peace of mind we are attempting to create with our meditation. We find the more attention we give the distractions the more they have a hold on us.

It is important to notice the difference between ignoring a problem by "pretending it is not there" as opposed to not feeding the problem. If we stop feeding the negativity, it might not completely go away, but it will begin to wither. This is not denial. We are making a choice to focus on what is working rather than focusing on what is not working. We are choosing to focus on a solution rather than the problem. We discover we do not need to feed the "bears" of negativity. They have already eaten our lunch; we do not have to give them our dinner as well.

Before I can make healthy choices for myself, I must be aware that I have the ability to choose. When I am not trapped in my negative thinking, I become aware that I do have choices. I will probably wrestle with the situation for awhile, but when I realize the futility of the struggle, I will make a decision. Although I can make the unhealthy choice of attempting to deny the situation, hopefully, I can allow myself to be open to the lesson and the blessing.

As we open ourselves to learning life's lessons we can also ask another meaningful question when faced with difficult situations: "How am I going to hold this?" We have a choice how we respond or how we hold the sometimes thorny things of life. We can hold them either as disasters or as lessons.

Occasionally, I will get together with a few friends and we will put together some music for church. Melba, a wonderful vocalist and musician, introduced us to an old Baptist hymn called *It Is Well with My Soul*. We loved the melody, the first verse and chorus, so we worked it up as an introduction to meditation. Melba then filled us in on the history of the hymn. It was written by Horatio Gates Spafford, who lost his son and much of his fortune during the great Chicago fire, but he, along with some others, spent two years working diligently with the destitute and homeless. He was persuaded to take some time off, and he planned a trip with his wife and four daughters. They went on before him, and the ship sank, killing all four of his children. The story almost sounded like Job, but unlike Job, after all of this, Spafford wrote the hymn, *It Is Well with My Soul*. I am in awe of that faith which clutched this angel of pain and death and said "I will not let you go until you bless me."

Sometimes I do not know, or I might never know, the blessing on a material level. My faith in a loving God tells me that good will somehow come from this. I might not see it, but it will come.

When we pray, "I will not let you go until you bless me," we realize that we do not have to be a victim of circumstance. Things will happen in our lives that we have little or no control over. Instead of trying to throw them away or deny them, we embrace them as a part of life; we release them to God, and we also learn from them. We open ourselves to the learning and blessing our life experience has for us.

The blessing comes from my willingness to surrender to a higher wisdom, the wisdom of God, so that I might learn and grow. At times the lesson will be revealed to me in human terms. Other times the lesson is a mystery, and the learning I do is on a deep level of faith. In faith, I let go, surrender, and know the blessing is there even if I cannot perceive it.

Seeking the blessing in what we are experiencing is not limited to outside events and circumstances. There is a deep metaphysical truth that nothing transforms until we first embrace it, and further, nothing transforms within us until we first embrace it as a part of ourselves.

There are many issues we struggle with within ourselves such as addictions, attachments, resentments, blame, shame, guilt, and a host of other conflicting elements. Again, our initial response is to deny that those negative energies really belong to us, to try to throw them away or to blame someone else for them. We hold to the false hope that they will go away or stop being a problem if we pretend they are not there. We find it is only by embracing those troubling things as being a part of ourselves that transformation occurs.

In the language of recovery: "We admitted we were powerless..." Until that admission, there was always someone or something else to blame. Another paradox of surrender is that when we are willing to admit our powerlessness, the powerlessness of the ego, we have opened the door to transformation. If there is something about ourselves we desire to change, we must first embrace it as part of ourself. It is in loving ourselves where we are, and as we are, that opens the door to transformation.

Using love to transform is drastically different from the ego's method of taking on change. If you want to lose weight, for example, the ego's method is to have you strip and stand in front of a mirror. After a huge dose of blame, shame, and guilt, and when you can no longer stand to look at yourself anymore, then, according to the ego, you are genuinely motivated. The catch is that this method only works for a short time. This is one of the major reasons diets and New Year's resolutions only last upwards to thirty-six hours. Guilt is a great short-term motivator, but does not and cannot last. Blame, shame, and guilt make us feel rotten enough to want to change, but they do not contain the energy to promote change; they only supply the desire. Desire without the means to attain the goal can be more destructive than no motivation at all.

The energy of Spirit encourages me to embrace and love myself where I am. If I want to get in better shape, I first love myself in the shape I am in. I do not have to love the shape I am in, but I do have to love myself as a size sixteen or forty-two waist, or whatever measurement is making me crazy. This is not denial nor is it the acceptance of unhealthy behavior. By expressing love rather than shame, I love my body for being as healthy as it is and for functioning as well as it does. I am not trying to love my excess weight; I am loving myself.

The soul knows that when you open yourself to love as deeply as you can, you are allowing the energy of transformation to take over. When you love yourself in the present moment, you are taking your sense of self and bringing it to the Mind of God, which is the essence of love. As you consciously enter the awareness of the perfection that God already sees for you, then you will begin to treat your body perfectly and lovingly. The changes you desire will happen because the blueprint of God's loving perfection is already there.

By loving and embracing myself, and specifically in this case, my body, I allow myself to be able to perceive my body the way God perceives it, as perfect. "Well," you might say, "What good is that going to do if I want to change it?" The answer is, when I place my body in the Mind of God and give myself the opportunity to perceive it the way God perceives it, then I will begin to perceive it perfectly. What happens when I begin to perceive my body perfectly? I begin to treat it perfectly; I begin to love it perfectly; I begin to feed it perfectly; I begin to exercise it perfectly; I begin to do all the necessary things that are a reflection of love.

These changes that I want to happen in the physical world begin within myself. Then they begin to be more and more manifested in the external world because I am continuing to feed the notion that I dwell in the Divine Mind and in the presence of absolute love and perfection. When I perceive my body, or anything else, as dwelling in the Mind of God, I act as if it is perfect and my prayers begin to manifest.

As usual, the ego will present all kinds of objections. If there is an aspect of yourself you want to transform, the ego will tell you that you cannot legitimately love this part of yourself. The ego will offer all sorts of reasons. It will tell you: "This part of yourself (your weight, this habit, or compulsion) is unacceptable; you cannot love it." "If you do love it, it will stay with you forever." One of the most influential ego arguments that can get you off track is, "Well, you either embrace your (weight, size, habit, compulsion, attachment) now, or you can love it when it is under control; which is it? You can't have both."

Without getting into a fight with the ego, which is just what it wants, you can counter those arguments by opening to a deeper sense of truth. Imagine a healthy relationship with a child; you can love the child just as she is and at the same time encourage growth. There does not have to be a conflict between loving yourself as you are and being open to continuing transformation.

When you love and embrace an aspect of yourself, and take it in as being a part of you, you need to love it, but you do not have to like it. Take addictions, for example. You probably already know that as long as the addiction is "out there," as long as it is someone else's fault or problem, then nothing is going to change. It is only when you are willing to accept the addiction/attachment/compulsion as part of yourself that change begins to occur. It is only when you are willing to address the problem inside yourself and say, "This is me; this is my addiction" that the process of transformation begins. You do not have to like the habit, compulsion, or addiction, but you do have to take it in and embrace it as being part of yourself, for transformation to take place.

In Hindu sacred literature the mind and its ego-based voice is described as a drunken monkey. As much as I love that image, I find myself wanting to fight with the monkey rather than embrace him. Instead of the drunken monkey, a gentler image of the gibbering mind was offered by the spiritual teacher Jack Kornfield. He likens that ever-busy voice inside our minds to an undisciplined puppy. Since there are so many aspects of life that need to be embraced, I am inclined to be as gentle as possible. Old habits, mistaken attitudes, outdated beliefs, as well as aspects of myself I do not like very much, such as attachments and addictions, all must be embraced to be healed.

What do you do with an undisciplined puppy? You don't beat it up or throw it around. Even if you lose your patience once in a while you realize that yelling is useless. What you do is put the papers down, and you say "stay" or "sit" with the full knowledge and understanding the command is only going to last for a few seconds. Soon the puppy is going to be up and wandering around again. Then what do you do? You pick it up and put it on the papers again.

You might ask, "Well, how long do I have to do that?" I have concluded that I will be "puppy training" my mind until I do not have skin any more. If I realistically accept that my mind is going to go wandering off, I'm not going to judge it or make it into a terrible thing. It is going to be all right with me. The mind is just doing what minds do; the puppy is just doing what puppies do.

There is the puppy saying to itself, "Oh, here's something to eat; there's something to play with; there's something to tear up. I don't want to be here; I want to be over there." I pick it up and put it on the papers. The more I do that, the more I begin to realize what it is like to live in unconditional love and peace. I continue to treat all my being, including my wandering mind, with dignity, respect, and love.

I also take responsibility for my thoughts and actions. After all, it is my puppy. It is my mind. I might not like what it is doing, it might even annoy or anger me, but it is mine. This is not blaming or fault finding; it is acknowledgment of accountability. When I embrace and accept responsibility for a particular aspect of my life I wish to change, then I am truly open to the grace of transformation. I can practice this self-love even with things I do not like. I can say to myself, "Yes, this is mine; I own it; I am responsible for it," and in doing so I open the door to the powers of release and transformation.

Fairy tales abound with stories of transformation. *Beauty and the Beast* and *The Frog Prince* are just a few that demonstrate the principle of embracing-what-is in order to allow for transformation. Loving and embracing a person or a quality as it is, changes it for the better. A great metaphor for a saint is one who is continually kissing toads.

There are certainly times when our life experience will seem overwhelming. We might be faced with personal illness, the death or illness of a loved one, or financial or material loss. During those times it might be well-nigh impossible to seek out the blessing. At those instances it is wise to concentrate on seeking counsel and courage from God and others. Sometimes in the midst of our suffering and even beyond it we can find no love in the situation at all. At those times we are asked to open to the love within ourselves and allow that to guide us. When we begin to heal and get our lives back together, then we can begin to open to discover the blessing.

At the time I am writing our family is experiencing a deeply painful event. Our youngest granddaughter, Aoife (which is Gaelic for "Beautiful") has been diagnosed with a rare genetic illness which results in the deterioration of her nervous system. We are all in turmoil, and it is difficult for me to imagine what her parents are going through. Aoife is only four and a wonderful sweet spirit. So where is the lesson? Right now, I do not know. What I do know is that we are being asked to love her where she is now, not how she might be weeks or months from now. We are being asked not to get so lost in our feelings that we miss the gift of who she is at this moment. That is all we know now; perhaps later there will be other lessons, but for now we love her and love and support one another. Is it enough? I do not know; it is all we have. Does it take the pain away? No. Does it allow us to be free enough to live and love in the present moment? Yes.

There are times in the pain of the moment, as I am wrestling with the angel of these circumstances, I do not want to ask, "What is the lesson here?" I just want to cry and scream and yell at the unfairness of it all. I want to vent my anger towards God and the universe for this senseless outrage. "Why, Why, Why?" I ask, and there is no answer.

Although the question "Why?" is unanswerable, more meaningful questions do have answers. Instead of asking "Why?" which is an expression of the ego's outrage at not being in control, we can ask questions more essential to our being such as, "How can I heal?

How can I find the love in this? What would love do?" It is a question we can ask when confronted with any difficulty or confusion. "What would love do?"

Here is another profound learning. Surrender does not take the pain away. Letting go, however, does help us realize that even when we are in pain that is not all that is happening. We can also know we are not unique in our pain, nor are we alone in seeking and finding solace.

In the words of Ken Wilbur, "It is our work not to get rid of the waves on the ocean of life but to learn to surf." I would like to add that we are swimming, surfing, and sometimes floating in the ocean of God's infinite love.

MEDITATION: I WILL NOT LET YOU GO UNTIL YOU BLESS ME

As you get comfortable, relaxed, and open, take a few deep cleansing breaths, opening even more.

Count backwards from ten to one as you breathe deeply. You can feel a sense of lightness and receptiveness as you allow Spirit to speak to you, sharing with you exactly what you need.

As you relax, allow your attention to move towards something you consider being a problem in your life. Do not go through the list in your mind; simply let the thought of a difficulty come to you, as significant or insignificant as it might be.

Hold this problem or difficulty lightly. Think of it as an image you can hold in your hand. You can observe the whole thing, you can turn it this way and that. You are not analyzing, just noticing.

Take your time with this one.

Pause...

Now put it down, and allow these words to resonate within you, "What is the lesson here? What is it that I need to learn? What is this life situation teaching me?"

Just be quiet and be open. You might or might not get something right away, but you will, either now or later. Be open to however the learning comes to you. It could reveal itself in words, images, or sensations either now or later.

Pause...

If you choose to, say the words, "I will not let you go until you bless me."

Breathe and be open; breathe and be open.

Begin to be conscious again of your breathing. Breathe deeply and stretch. Come fully back here in your body, completely centered and grounded.

Get up, stretch, and look around you. Become familiar with the place again, feeling yourself in your body. Journal or process any other way you like.

NUGGETS

"I will not let you go until you bless me."

I have a choice of how I respond to life situations. I have a choice as to how I perceive them, and how I hold them.

I can learn from anything.

I depend on grace, the action of God's Love within me, to be my teacher.

When I let go, I do so cleanly. I not only let go of the situation and all it entails, I open myself to the lesson. I open myself to the learning. I open myself to becoming who I truly am.

We realize it is when we truly accept this situation of ours that transformation happens.

GRIEVING IS LETTING GO

BROWSING THROUGH my *favorite bookstore, my reverie is broken by a child crying. It was obvious she wanted something her mother was not going to buy. The sound of her crying pierces my soul and touches something primal inside of me; I want to weep as well. My tears are not only the expression of my own unfulfilled desires, they are also an expression of my sense of incompleteness and my sadness as I experience myself as separate and lost. The little girl's mother held her gently and firmly and asked her daughter in the most under-standing way, "Is your heart breaking?" to which the daughter replied a tearful "Yes." Mom then said lovingly "It will heal." It was a wonderful moment of grief, love, understanding, and healing.*

It is so easy to wrap ourselves around the pain when our heart is breaking. It is a huge challenge to push through the hurt and love with a broken heart.

The surrender of grieving is neither a denial of the pain of loss nor an attempt to cover the feelings of bereavement. Grieving is both moving through and moving beyond our experience of unexpected change, illness, loss, death, and all the other challenges life brings. Everything changes, goes away, or ends; that is the nature of the physical world. In order to cope with the loss and change in our lives, we grieve.

Everybody grieves, but since many of us live in an environment that does not accept or honor the feelings that are involved, much of our grieving is unconscious, discounted, or channeled in unhealthy ways. Because we do not learn that everything is transient, we do not learn that grieving is a natural process of life.

Everybody grieves, even children. When he loses a toy, or her ice cream cone falls on the ground, or the family has to move, the child grieves. When things go wrong, children can get stuck in the perception that life is unfair. Some people stay in that place all their lives. It requires learning, awareness, and openness to accept there is loss and that things change. These are unavoidable truths of life. Accepting the transitional nature of things, even physical life itself, allows people to be open to the process of grieving. When a person is open to walking through all the feelings of grief, they are also moving towards deeper healing and surrender.

We might hope that when we reach the point of surrender or letting go that our sadness will disappear, but that is not so. What we experience is not the evaporation of our feelings or a negation of them, but a state of mind where we are at peace with them. The sadness remains, but it is no longer overwhelming; the feelings of grief no longer control our lives.

At times of significant loss it is difficult to grasp how we can go on. It is equally difficult to understand how the world can go on. Grieving allows us to move from that global sense of pain to embracing our personal loss and moving forward. It is only when we allow ourselves to feel the hurt, the pain, the anger, and all the other feelings that might be part of the process for us that we can begin to move through that part of life. The fog lifts, just a bit, and we perceive there is more to us than our pain. We are open to knowing there is more to life than the crushing sadness we are experiencing.

I did not know anything about grieving for much of my life. I did not understand much about feelings at all. As I was coming to the end of my first year in recovery, and continuing to uncover all kinds of hulking phantoms lurking in the shadows and dusty corners of my psyche, I was also experiencing a newness and rebirth with a fresh sense of tenderness and vulnerability.

It was a year of struggle and challenge for me. I was growing into a new life. A different me was emerging, and I did not have the time or the energy to think about my process, or to even begin to understand it. A major portion of my energy went into not feeding my addiction. Whatever was left of my resources went into all that it takes for daily living such as going to work, making meetings, and taking care of the normal everyday things most people take for granted. In my self-absorption, I felt these Herculean efforts on my part deserved a huge reward. Someone kindly reminded me I was simply doing what I was supposed to be doing all along!

Towards the end of that year, I was at a conference exploring spiritual matters, and one of the speakers was expounding on the (then) new work of Elizabeth Kubler-Ross on death and dying. As the speaker began to describe the stages of death, which later became known as the stages of grief, I began to see myself in all of them and became deeply aware of what my journey over the past year had entailed. As she described the simplified version of the five stages of grief which consisted of Denial, Bargaining, Anger/Humiliation, Depression, and Acceptance/Surrender, I was blown away. The whole past year, and a little time before my recovery, flashed right through me, and a clearer picture emerged. I had not died a physical death, but these stages of grief were my process as well.

I was amazed at the parallels and talked about them energetically with those I was with, and then I began to put grieving into the larger context of letting go and surrender. I was beginning to realize grieving was a process that was related to many areas of life, not just dying.

Even though surrender and letting go in the form of grieving is such a significant factor in my life, I still often lose touch with it. Consequently, I will discover myself caught up in denial more often than I would like. Denial can manifest as blame, projection onto another, or sometimes I will simply pretend the situation is not happening at all. Other times I will be caught up in anger at myself, the universe, God, or all three. I will find myself trying to control and manipulate something that is beyond my power to do anything about.

I need to remind myself that grieving is an essential process of life because it is so easy to get stuck in my experiences of denial, anger, and depression. Change is an inevitable aspect of living in a world of matter, and grieving is a process that permeates my life.

The following is a brief refresher course on the process of grief. The first stage of grieving is denial. Denial with addictions, for example, could express itself in ways such as, "I really don't have a problem. Everything would be all right if my partner, boss, family would just get a grip and straighten out." Of course, to the person in denial, straightening out means, "If they would just get off my back and let me do exactly what I wanted to do, then I would not have a problem." During this stage there is just flat-out not seeing the problem as a problem. The shock of a death or severe loss leads the psyche to cushion the blow by saying things such as, "I just talked with her yesterday." "No, that can't be: we were going to have lunch next week." "We had just been making plans for this trip."

A little window opens when we enter the next phase called bargaining. We begin to realize that denial is no longer working; we begin to recognize we have a problem. We are beginning to be conscious that a situation needs our attention, even though we are not even close to perceiving its significance. The bargaining mind and ego might put it this way: "I have a problem, but..." "Perhaps if I move to a different place, get a different job, a different house, a different wife/husband, a different face, a different name, a different..."

When I move past bargaining, I have to make much more of a conscious choice. I could remain in denial or bargaining for the rest of my life, as many people do. If I choose to move through the mental bargaining phase, I begin to feel rage and helplessness or what is referred to as the Anger/Humiliation stage of grieving. Some expressions of this stage are: "God, why did you do this to me?" "God, why did you let this happen?" "What am I going to do?" "Just leave me alone."

If it is death we are dealing with, then we can become angry with the person for leaving. We can be angry at God, or angry at ourselves for all the pieces of unfinished business we have. We can be angry at not making the best of all the opportunities we had or all the above and more. The thinking mind wants to make sense of it all, and it cannot. It is from the mind's frustration that anger also arises. "I don't know; I don't understand. I am angry that I do not know, and that I do not understand." Anger flows from the sense of lack of control, helplessness, and a sense of the unfairness of it all.

Although anger many times is a cover emotion for hurt, fear, or guilt, it remains a very powerful energy that needs to be expressed, perhaps by yelling, screaming, or beating pillows. I know that when I get the physical edge off the anger, the tears are bound to follow. Even after all the workshops and sophisticated learning I have been through, one of my favorite methods for releasing anger remains one of the simplest. I roll up the windows of my car and scream my bloody lungs out. The release relieves the heaviness and inertia in my guts, and rather than those feelings turning into depression, I am now able to experience the pain of my grief, and I can allow it to move through me.

Before surrender or acceptance comes depression. (This is not what is psychologically referred to as clinical depression. That is a very different issue and requires professional treatment.) When I first consciously experienced this stage of grief, I had been masking my feelings for so long, I do not think I had any idea what I was feeling. Before I was committed to working on myself, around bargaining time, a friend of mine asked me how I was doing. I replied, "I'm doing OK." He looked at me and said something I will never forget, "I don't think you know what OK feels like." Those words jolted me, woke me up, hurt like hell, and got me moving. Finally, I was beginning to feel everything I had never allowed myself to feel for years.

Much of my depression comes from frozen or unexpressed anger, and much of the anger felt in the grieving process has been unexpressed for years. If I learn not to feel, one of the biggest things I learn not to feel is anger. Some of the inner dialogue around this stage might express itself as, "I'm stuck"; "I'm never going to get out of here"; "I thought I felt bad before; this is worse"; "Nothing is ever going to change." For me, this stage of grief took on a heaviness and lethargy I did not know how to shake off. I felt as if I were an insect trapped in amber or a survivor from a lost safari attempting to walk through a mire of quicksand. Along with the heaviness and lethargy, I also experienced the vague promise of an approaching daybreak. A realization began to dawn on me, like sunlight peeking around a corner. The realization was, I have all these feelings, I am responsible for them, but they are not who I am. Surrender reveals this truth even more fully to me.

The final stage in grieving is simply referred to as surrender. Other terms which express different flavors of this finishing stage are acceptance, letting go, or detachment.

As I continued to absorb and understand the process of grieving, I began to become more and more aware of how much of a role it plays in all of our lives. Every time I change, even if it is simply changing my mind, from one simple thought or idea to another, this whole process of grieving takes place. I am constantly going through this, sometimes with big things in my life, and often with little things as well. Life is a constant taking in and letting go, a constant grieving and embracing, a succession of hellos and goodbyes.

Even letting go of things we no longer want to keep requires grieving. That is difficult to realize at times, but it is true. One of the reasons old habits, thoughts, or ideas do not leave us as readily as we would like is that we have not grieved. "Hidden grieving" is the grief we need to process even when we lose something we want to lose.

Imagine that a new neighbor moves in next door. The person is loud, unruly, throws parties all the time; obnoxious people are constantly coming and going out of the house. There is a constant racket along with police cars and sirens on weekends. The person also has a dog the size of a pony who loves to tear open your garbage, and seems to think your lawn and driveway are his exclusive toilet.

As it turns out, having a neighbor like this takes up a lot of time and energy. The energy that goes into protecting your garbage; keeping the dog out of your yard; tossing the dog poop over the fence; your complaining to the police; you and your neighbors petitioning to get this person out of there is huge.

There could also be some great coffee-break and family conversations beginning with: "Wait until you hear this one." "Well, I thought last week was awful, you should hear what happened this week." "Did I tell you about the one my neighbor pulled yesterday?" "Hi, honey, I'm home; what happened next door today?"

Imagine next that something happens, either the neighbor gets carted off to jail, is shot, or simply moves away. The house is now empty, the neighbor and dog are gone, you and your family return to your normal state of quiet living, but then you notice something is missing. All that energy that used to be directed at the neighbor is now sitting there doing nothing; you might even find there is not much to talk about any more. You are out of practice with your normal topics of sharing. At work, you used to be the life of the party. Everyone looked forward to your outlandish stories of your neighbor's exploits. You did not realize it, but you enjoyed the limelight and the attention. You were something special, now you are back to being average again. When anyone asks you what is going on, instead of having a string of stories to tell, the response now is, "Oh, not much." That hole, that empty space is healed by grieving.

Surprising, but true: I need to grieve all my losses, even grieving the things I wanted to get rid of in the first place.

We would also like to be rid of old patterns of behavior, attitudes, and outdated ideas which no longer serve us. Whether we like it or not these attachments have become part of us, and letting them go or changing them involves loss, and loss must always be grieved for the change to take place. We even need to give up things that have only happened in our minds such as dreams and expectations. I need to grieve for all my losses.

In speaking with clients who have experienced a breakup in a relationship, I have noticed many people are confused when they discover they are still holding onto something or someone that they know is gone. What we mutually discovered is that they are still unconsciously holding onto the dream of what that relationship could be. As long as they are holding onto that dream or that fantasy, they are not going to be able to grieve and let go. When grieving seems to get stuck, check it out to see if there is not a fantasy or piece of fantasy around it you are still holding onto.

Sometimes grieving can be expressed on even deeper levels. At times, grieving can touch the soul and the psyche on a mythic level. Many of us grew up with the Judeo-Christian story of the Garden of Eden. Eden was a perfect place where the Light and Love of God were ever present. Then Adam and Eve were cast out of the Garden. We were thrown into this imperfect world where many times God does not feel or appear that close, needs are not met and, more often than not, things are not perfect and many times not even fair.

There is a time to grieve and then a time to move on. There is a time to embrace, accept, surrender, and take the risk to grow.

I grieve being cast out of the Garden over and over again. There is a realization in me of how things could be, and when I contrast that with how things are, I grieve. I sometimes feel as if I am adrift and dispossessed. I remember a friend of mine commented to me after watching the movie *ET*, "Everyone I talked with thought ET was so cute they just wanted to take him home with them. Not me. I wanted none of that. I wanted to get in that space ship of his and *go home!*"

So for some of us, like my want-to-go-home friend and I, there is an intense grieving about being here in this physical world. I feel it is important that I recognize the grieving, but not become caught up in it. There is a time to grieve and then a time to move on. There is a time to embrace, accept, surrender, and take the risk to grow. I can also know that my grieving the loss of perfection is my hunger for union with God as well.

Although the surrender of grieving is a continual thread running through life's tapestry, there is nothing trivial about it. There are times of such intense and deep grieving that it is difficult to understand why everyone does not feel the way I feel. "Why is the world still turning?" "Why are people still going to work, acting as if nothing is happening?" I can even find myself resentful of another's joy and happiness. When I first received word of our granddaughter's illness, every time I saw a mother and little girl together laughing or having a good time, I would feel sadness. I would especially feel angry if I heard a mother yelling at a kid. I would think, "Don't you realize how precious this person is? Don't you realize how precious this moment is? What are you doing wasting it?"

In the midst of grief nothing except our pain seems to have any meaning or purpose, yet life does go on, we are still here. There are sinks to be cleaned, meals to eat, jobs to do, people to love, and gifts to receive. As we walk through the valley of our pain and loss continuing to do the necessary things of life, even if we do them mechanically, there will be an occasional moment that will make us smile, despite ourselves. We will inadvertently laugh at a joke or a funny story; we might even remember our loved one with a fond memory that brings joy.

If we allow the process to lovingly unfold, the other side of grieving can reveal a deeper heart, more compassionate, and more ready to forgive.

MEDITATION: RELEASING GRIEF

As you get comfortable, relaxed, and open;
take a few deep cleansing breaths, opening
even more.

Count backwards from ten to one as you breathe deeply. You can feel a sense of lightness and receptiveness as you allow Spirit to speak to you, sharing with you exactly what you need.

Breathe deeply and experience yourself more and more relaxed as you open to this meditation.

We all have grief inside of us. This is a time to release and let go.

As you relax there might be a particular grieving issue in your life you need to let go of that comes up or you might just feel the sadness that needs to be released with no specific context. Either one or a mixture of both is OK.

Feel where you feel it in your body. Is it tight; does it have tears; are there any other emotions connected with it?

Notice all of it and allow yourself to be as willing as you can to let it move through you and release.

Pause...

Just be open to the process, there is nothing you need to force or make happen.

Breathe into wherever you feel all of that inside you, and as you breathe into it, allow it to release. Let go of any expectations you might have as to how or when that release is going to happen. Just breathe and be open to release. If tears come, let them come. If there are other feelings, breathe into them and release.

There is no need to force anything. Let the cleansing and healing power of the Spirit of God move with you and through you, healing and releasing. Healing and releasing.

Know that this process might continue within you. You might experience more or deeper release at other times. You will know that it is happening. It does not need to be disturbing. The Spirit of God is with you, healing.

When some of these sensations arise again, breathe into them and let them go.

Know that your process will continue. As life flows there will be both joy and sorrow. Hold them both gently.

Breathe.

Begin to be conscious again of your breathing. Breathe deeply and stretch. Come fully back here in your body, completely centered and grounded.

Get up, stretch, and look around you. Become familiar with the place again, feeling yourself in your body. Journal or process any other way you like.

NUGGETS

My grieving is not limited to the serious and important issues of life. I can be engulfed with a sense of loss over the first scratch on a new car or my lost keys or even the cover of a new book that gets bent by accident.

Grieving can be a measure of my love in the best sense and the level of my attachment in a more unhealthy way.

When a beloved object gets scratched or dented, I might be grieving my loss of perfection rather than the object itself.

Denial happens much more than we think. That's why it's called denial.

Sadness is truly a bitter-sweet emotion. I never quite push it away completely, nor do I want to.

Anger is often a cover emotion for the more vulnerable feelings I have such as hurt, fear, or shame. Expressing those underlying feelings would make me feel even more vulnerable. When we feel threatened by vulnerability, anger can appear to be a powerful protector.

PRAYER IS SURRENDER

WHEN I PRAY, *"God, I do not know the answer. You do. Please show me; I am willing,"* I let go of my will. I open myself to the power of God flowing through me. I empty myself and allow myself to be filled with the power of God.

I like to think of myself as being very spiritual, but there are times when prayer is the last act that comes to my mind. When a life situation grabs me, and I become angry and overwhelmed, I am either frantically attempting to fix something or I am stuck in a morass of funk where there is no solution. The phrase, "When all else fails, pray!" has special relevance to me. As I continue on the path, I want to make prayer the first thing I think of rather than the last.

In order to allow prayer and my connection with God to be a priority, there are some old images and ideas which need to be brought to consciousness and transformed. My outdated image of prayer would appear something like this: I would be on my knees broadcasting the hopes, desires, and pleadings of my heart sometimes in words, sometimes not. There would be this huge beacon "up there" that picked up my transmissions and the countless prayers of everyone else. Then these signals would be fed into this huge ultimate-computer-like thing. God would then sort through all this stuff and decree how a particular prayer request would be dealt with. The typical answers I would expect were, "Yes," "No," "Maybe," and "Wait." Prayer was similar to consulting the "Magic 8 Ball" or to tossing a coin into a fountain. Prayer was a bit like a crap shoot. Sometimes you win; sometimes you lose. You put your money (prayer request) in the machine and hope you hit a "winner."

In our old vision, if we or someone else had a need such as a job, money, or healing, we would send this request to God. God was this energy or this big invisible person who processed all these desires. So God receives our prayer request and decides whether to give us what we ask for or not. If our prayer is acceptable we get what we requested: the new car, the job, victory in the football game, selling the house, or healing for our mother. We were told that God could also answer prayer by saying, "No." So as wonderful and heartfelt as our prayer might have been, according to this model, "No" might be the best answer we could get.

Newscasts of natural disasters, such as a fire or earthquake, will sometimes portray this very limited notion of God and prayer. When survivors are interviewed many will say, "God was looking out for us." Of course, the unspoken presumption is that God was not looking out for those who were killed or whose homes were destroyed. That kind of reasoning never made much sense to me, and it certainly did not seem to reflect a loving, caring God either.

Today I know God is not a gigantic invisible person in the sky who loves me; God is Love. God is the creative power of the universe that exists everywhere and infuses everything. God does not *have* all the qualities we attribute to God; God *is* the living embodiment of those qualities. God is Light; God is Wisdom; God is Strength; God is Creativity; God is Compassion. God is all of those qualities, and most of all, God is Love. Even though learning and experience have taught me all this, my old ideas are almost reflexive in their resilience. Although I know that prayer is the awakening to the God-force within me, instead of focusing inward, I still find myself occasionally looking to a heaven "up there" someplace and waiting for some outside force to pull me out of the soup.

The healthier and more workable model of prayer comes from an awareness of the power of God that dwells within us. The notion that this power is within all of us is supported by mystics and scripture from all major forms of belief. Sikhism states, "Even as the scent dwells within the flower, so God (is) within thine own heart (and) ever abides." The Qua'ran states, "I have breathed into man My spirit." In Hindu scripture, it is stated, "God bides hidden in the hearts of all." Shintoism asserts, "Do not search in distant skies for God, in man's own heart he is found."

According to Christian scripture, "For lo, the kingdom of God is within you." (Lk 17:21); "I pray that God will help you overflow with hope in him through the Holy Spirit's power within you." (Ro 15:13); "Know ye not that ye are a temple of God, and that the Spirit of God dwelleth in you?" (1 Co 3:16); "Christ is not weak in his dealings with you, but is a mighty power within you." (2 Co 13:3); "For God is at work within you." (Phil 2:13); "Guard well the splendid, God-given ability you received as a gift from the Holy Spirit who lives within you." (2 Ti 1:14); "But you have received the Holy Spirit and he lives within you." (1 Jn 2:27); "Last of all I want to remind you that your strength must come from the Lord's mighty power within you." (Eph 6:10). These scriptures are not speaking about the ego "me"; they are referring to the spiritual aspect of my being that is created in the image and likeness of God.

Here is a secret: No matter what you might be thinking or feeling, you are always in God. You are always in God, even when you do not feel it. You are always in God, even when you are not conscious of it. You can never be outside of the Presence of God's Love. It would be like walking outside and say-

> **Here is a secret: No matter what you might be thinking or feeling, you are always in God. You are always in God, even when you do not feel it. You are always in God even when you are not conscious of it.**

ing, "I'm not going to let the sun shine on me today." Well, try as you might, the sun is going to shine on you anyway. You can pretend the sun is not shining on you, but it is shining on you nonetheless. A prayer from the Unity tradition is a wonderful reminder of the inner power of prayer: "The Light of God surrounds us; the Love of God enfolds us; the Power of God protects us; and the Presence of God watches over us. Wherever we are, God is." In prayer, we consciously align ourselves with the Power of God, both inside ourselves and outside.

When I am "down here" and God is "up there," I have to work on getting my prayer perfect so God really hears it. I lose touch with Jesus' message concerning prayer, "Do not heap up empty phrases, as the Gentiles do, thinking you will be heard by many words. Do not be like them; your Father knows what you need before you ask him." (Mt 6:7-8 NRSV) I find those words very consoling.

Prayer, uniting my power with the power of God, opens me to the transformational power of love. That power not only changes my perspective on life, the power of God's love also frees me. In the flow of God's love, I open myself to transformation.

In the Garden of Gethsemane, Jesus prayed, "Not my will (the will of my ego), but Yours (the will of God) be done." (Lk 22:42) This moving beyond the limited and constricting will of my ego to a joining of my will and God's will is also beautifully voiced in the language of recovery. The 11th Step states we "sought to improve our conscious contact with God, praying only for God's will for us and the power to carry that out." We do not simply surrender; we also open ourselves to be guided by the Will of Spirit. We pray. We put the concern into God's hands. We open ourselves to the solution. We realize that the answer to our prayer might direct us on a partic-ular course of action. We pray for a positive outcome. We not only let go of the matter into God's hands, but we pray for the power, ability, and knowledge to be able to do whatever it is we are called upon to do in this situation.

God *always* answers prayer, and I have responsibilities as well. One of them is to be open as to how my prayer will be answered. I do not want to become attached to the form I think the answer should take. My human consciousness is limited. Even though I think I know how my prayer should be answered, that does not necessarily mean my desire is the best possible outcome. The fact is, I probably would not be praying if I already knew the best possible outcome. When I have a set idea of what the answer to my prayer will be, I become too attached to the form of the answer, and if I am just looking in one direction I might miss the answer when it does show up.

There is an old joke about a man trapped in a flood. He climbs to the roof of his home to get away from the rising waters, and he prays to God to save him. Soon a rowboat comes by, and a rescue worker asks him to get in. The guy on the roof says, "No, God will save me." Well, another boat comes by and then a helicopter. The guy responds the same way, "No, God is going to save me." The waters rise and he drowns. As he reaches the Pearly Gates he angrily confronts God about not answering his prayer. God calmly replies, "Joe, I sent you two rowboats and a helicopter. What more did you want?" I often wonder how many "rowboats" I have missed when I have been looking for something else.

There is often an unconscious side to our prayer. Many times this hidden aspect is the assumption or expectation that God will do "it" for us, that all we need to do is ask. A prayer with its hidden agenda uncovered might sound something like this: "God, fix my life, but don't ask me to change." My prayer could be more global in scope, "God, please God, fix the world, but please don't ask me to sacrifice anything. Change them not me."

Because prayer is a joining of the mind and heart to God, there is also action required on my part. When recovery programs suggest that "God is doing for us what we could not do for ourselves," that is not a suggestion to simply lie on the floor after we have prayed and wait for the miracle. Our God can do anything. There is nothing God cannot do. That is true, and that truth is tempered by the gospel incident at Jesus' hometown of Nazareth, when it was stated, "Because they did not have faith, he did not perform many miracles there." (Mt 13:58) Why is it that our prayer does not come to fruition? At times it is because we cannot yet hold the belief that our prayer can or will be answered. At times, making room for our prayer to be answered means being open to the highest reality we can hold at this moment. One of the ways that prayer works is by manifesting, through the power of God, the highest reality we can see now. We hold a loving space for the miracle to happen.

There have been times in my life when I have felt deeply depressed. Although I wanted to be wildly happy and carefree, in my depressed state of mind I just could not hold the image of myself as outrageously joyous and free. If I was broke or struggling with finances, I could have prayed that I become fantastically wealthy and have so much money I will never be fearful or experience lack ever again. That image is so far from the truth as I see it now, I would probably have a very difficult time wrapping myself around it. What I can do is ask myself, "What is the highest reality I can see now?" Maybe it is getting out of bed instead of pulling the covers over my head. Maybe it is cleaning my room; maybe it is going to a meeting or praying, or surrendering; maybe it is thinking of myself as having enough money to buy enough food to fill me up and even to have a little left over to rent a movie. Let my prayer be, "God, let me hold to the highest reality of this need (peace, happiness, prosperity) and through Your power and grace within me allow my vision to grow."

On a global scale, when you think about the Middle East, for example, can you imagine peace there? I know you want to, but can you really hold an image of Israelis and Palestinians living in harmony, sharing Jerusalem in peace? As soon as you attempt to hold that image of peace and calm, the vision of angry faces and car bombs exploding can intrude. When negative images or ideas begin to interfere with my positive vision, I let my mind go back to an image of a Palestinian or Israeli grieving over the loss of a loved one, and then I can realize all people have the same feelings I do; they are not separate from me. I might create the image of two people from different countries embracing one another. I might not be able to see the countries at peace, but I can see two people at peace.

I begin with that. As soon as I become lost in the same quagmire of fear and hopelessness that grips much of that part of the world, I remind myself I do not have to hold the entire vision of peace yet. Let me begin with a simple peaceful image of brother loving brother. Let me do that for a few seconds, and know that by holding that simple image, I am contributing to the larger manifestation of total peace. This is one way I cooperate with grace and become a co-creator with God.

Another responsibility in prayer is to make room for the answers to come through. As we examine ourselves and dedicate ourselves more fully to life in the Spirit, we begin to discover the kinds of thinking we are holding onto that are frustrating our experience of the flow of love, grace, and the good.

Do you ever remember praying, "Please, oh please, God, get me out of this; I'll never do it again?" I do not wish to disparage those prayers. These prayers of desperation are sometimes the most honest prayers we have ever spoken. We are surrendering; we are opening to the infinite power of God. We might not always be conscious of it in these moments, but we are surrendering. It is a deep and heartfelt letting go. Difficulty arises when we get out of the jam and just go back to doing the same things over again.

There was a movie years ago called *The End,* and all the way through it Burt Reynolds is trying to commit suicide. He finally decides to swim out in the ocean as far as he can and then just sink and drown. He swims out until he is exhausted and then as he is going down for the second time he has a revelation; he really wants to live, so he desperately struggles back to the surface and prays, "Oh, God, if you just get me to shore I will give everything I have to the poor." He receives this tremendous surge of energy and gets closer and closer to shore. His prayer now is, "Oh, God, if you save me I will give *half* of what I own to the poor." It is a funny story, but all too true for most of us if our surrender is based on situations more than true willingness to change.

"To You, O Lord, I lift up my soul." (Ps 25:1 NRSV)

In prayer, I choose to be in conscious contact with God. I choose to identify with my spiritual nature rather than my ego. I literally bring to consciousness the presence of God in my life and all my surroundings. A powerful way of continually being aware of the presence of God is acknowledging God working in my life, not just with the nice things that have happened, not just the prosperity that showed up, but in everything. Everything that occurs in my life is the energy of God, loving, teaching, healing, and stretching me. Jung succinctly expressed it when he said, "God is all that happens to me, all that crosses my path, which is filled with surprise for which I am totally unprepared or not expecting."

Prayer is letting go of a sense of scarcity or lack. There is a realization in prayer that love is abundant and boundless; there are no limits to grace. "Wait and see," says the fearful mind. When I am in a state of mind that is just waiting for someone or something to change, nothing happens. I see those non-productive "waiting" dynamics so often in couples therapy. "If only you would change that behavior, then I would change this, but I'm not willing to change unless you are." On a larger scale we have a similar dynamic with nations that are sworn enemies. There is the unwritten fear that there is not going to be enough love or compassion to go around. The fear expresses itself as: "I had better protect what I have, and not give you any until I am guaranteed you will give me some of yours." On a spiritual level that kind of thinking is ridiculous. It is similar to being afraid that God is going to run out of love, or mercy, or compassion. When I am in scarcity and fear waiting for you to make a move, nothing is going to happen, but when I see you as a child of God, and when I know I am a child of God as well, that is when transformation happens. It is only then that the power of God, which is always present, can flow through me and into the situation.

When we "lift up our soul," we are raised above the problem. Being raised above the problem does not mean our feelings disappear. We pray that we do not allow our feelings to govern our perception. In the Lord's Prayer we pray, "On earth as it is in heaven." We are praying to let go of our limited view here on this earthly plane, because we know the "earth consciousness" is the consciousness of separation. We ask that the consciousness of limitation and separation be replaced by the consciousness of Heaven, the consciousness of Oneness. We realize that when we think we are separate, we are afraid. When we are in Oneness, we are in Love.

When I pray "Lord, let me see peace instead of this," it does not mean, "God, You have to make this whole thing stop and I will see peace." No. What prayer ignites in me is the sense that when I see peace all of this other conflict will stop. My prayer is not just for things to disappear, but for a change of heart, an emotional change in perception to occur. Then, through grace, I can come to the realization that my perception is a choice. It is a choice of what I focus on. As in that beautiful couplet from Frederick Langbridge, "Two men looked out from prison bars, one saw mud the other stars." Looking at the stars does not make the mud disappear, but I have a choice of where I center my attention. New Testament scripture has a wonderful parallel to the mud-and-stars choice. There were two thieves crucified with Jesus. One is loudly complaining, wrapped up in his own suffering (by the way, I can't blame him, I might be doing the same thing), and the other, sometimes referred to as St. Dismas, the good thief, reaches out to Jesus and asks for forgiveness. "One saw mud the other stars." This is the choice of perception and the power to choose given to us through prayer.

"You even lift me above those who rise up against me; You rescue me from the violent man." (2 S 22:49 NASB)

There are times when I might not be able to lift up my soul. I can experience myself as constricted, helpless, and overwhelmed. My prayer might be one of an even deeper surrender when I ask God to do the lifting up. At times such as these my prayer might be, "Lord, raise me up above the craziness." I sometimes recall that beautiful song, *You Raise Me Up*. There is such a sense of power and love in that piece of music. It is also wonderful to recognize it is not a song of denial about what is happening; it is not pretending everything is la-la land. It is a deeper realization that the crisis, pain, or suffering is not everything. There is a deeper or higher reality. There is a reality above the chaos and indifference, above the anger and fear, and above the hatred and revenge.

The Prodigal Son said, "I will arise and go to my father." (Lk 15:11-32) He did not say, "Oh, the pigs will just disappear, and all of my past mistakes will be wiped from my consciousness." No. He did, however, create a level of awareness which made clear that, "The pigs are here; the hunger is here; the despair is here, but I can move. I do not have to choose to stay here. I will get up. I will remove myself from this situation. I will shift my focus from my dire circumstances to the love of my father. I am not denying what is going on here; I am choosing to focus on a deeper truth."

We can embrace the answer to prayer and connecting to the power of God on a material level, or a deeper level of Spirit. Certainly rescuing me from violence is important, but even more so is the "lifting up." Jesus saw no cripples. He saw everyone as whole. Because His perception of wholeness was much more powerful than anyone else's negative perception, He literally raised up those whom others saw as blind or lame. Jesus raised them up to a vibrational level above sickness and disease. He lifted them up to a level of consciousness that reflected wholeness and health. This is another reason why Jesus so many times equated healing with the forgiveness of sins. Sin is the separator. When He forgave sin He was saying, "I remove the vibration and sense of separation. I remove this; I do not see it in you. Neither do I condemn you. I raise you up above the vibrational level of sickness to another consciousness. I see you as the Father sees you. I see you as love."

MEDITATION: PRAYER

As you get comfortable, relaxed, and open,
take a few deep cleansing breaths, opening even more.

Count backwards from ten to one as you breathe deeply.
You can feel a sense of lightness and receptiveness as you allow Spirit
to speak to you, sharing with you exactly what you need.

Breathe deeply and experience yourself more and more relaxed as you open to this meditation.

Prayer is not simply talking to God.

Prayer is consciously connecting to God, the source. It is recognizing the source; it is opening to the source.

As you relax and go deeper, imagine that you are surrounded by white light. It is a light that is so real that it almost has a physical sense and texture about it. You are surrounded by it. This marvelous white light is surrounding you, and upholding you. You can even breathe it in. Try it; breathe it in and allow it to touch every cell and fiber of your being, physically, mentally, emotionally, and spiritually.

This light is the unconditional love of God that upholds and surrounds you. God is your source. God is your source for everything. The energy of God surrounds and upholds you.

Pause...Breathe

No matter what it is you feel that you need, whether it is health, money, forgiveness, strength; whatever it is you need, God is your source.

Notice within yourself what is calling to you–healing, nurturing, abundance. Let whatever it is come to your consciousness. You do not have to think about it. Just let it come. Allow these needs and these desires of your heart to rest on this altar of light that surrounds you. Let go of them into the unconditional love of God.

Breathe, rest, and know your prayer is heard and is being answered in this instant.

Let go of how you think the answer should appear. Trust and know.

Pause...

Breathe, stretch. Thank you, God.

Begin to be conscious again of your breathing. Breathe deeply and stretch. Come fully back here in your body, completely centered and grounded.

Get up, stretch, and look around you. Become familiar with the place again, feeling yourself in your body. Journal or process any other way you like.

NUGGETS

Oh, Lord raise me up. I can't see a path out of this. Lord, help me to see.

Raise me above my limitations. Raise me above my belief in my limitations.

It is wonderful to know God is within us, but when we are overwhelmed we cannot see or know or be open to the experience of God in us. It is then we must remind ourselves that God is all around us–everywhere.

Nothing is too big for God, but let us begin our prayer from where we are.

I want to pray for a world at peace. Let me start with holding the door for the next person I meet.

If any intention seems too big to hold, let me start simply.

Let me remember although a situation might be too big for me, it is not too big for God. So my prayer might be "God, it's too big, I can't hold the vision." Then God says, "I've been waiting to hear you say that. If it is too big for you, that is what I am here for."

"Lord of Light, Love, and Truth, there are times when I am overwhelmed with the immensity of the craziness of this world. I don't want to feel this pain, but I also know the world's pain and conflict is my pain and conflict. Open me to the peace of knowing I am a channel of Your Love and Wisdom. Flow through me. Flow through me, Oh God, until there is only You. Thank you, God. Amen."

Fixing and controlling do not work because there is always something else to be fixed or controlled.

When I first surrender, I might feel like a victim again. I mistakenly think my surrender is a reflection of my powerlessness. It is not. My surrender is an expression of my *ego's* powerlessness. When I accept the things I cannot change, the truth I am accepting is that I cannot change them the way I have been trying to change them. In the past I was dependent on the power of my ego to change my life; in surrender I am allowing the power of God to make the changes.

Of all the harmful thoughts and behaviors we have grown attached to, nothing is more destructive than the negative thinking we have created about ourselves.

Surrender in prayer and other areas of life does not happen just once. It happens again and again and again.

In the Sixties we sang, "We shall overcome…" We shall overcome violence, hatred, oppression, bigotry, and prejudice. We will not battle it or those who produce it, but by the power of God we will overcome it.

What is it that I am giving to God? I am giving God the outcome, the form the miracle will take. I might not ever understand it. I release the results into God, and I continue to pray for the grace to deal with whatever happens.

Our serenity is inversely proportional to our expectations.

SADNESS AND SURRENDER

FINALLY THE TEARS CAME. *On the face of it, I cried with feelings of anger, sadness, and helplessness over a good friend being treated unfairly. In truth, the tears embodied the submerged grief of a lifetime, from the loneliness of adolescence, the devastation of addictions, and the loss of my parents. It was painful. It was healing.*

Life wisdom comes from experiences, not words. I continue to learn there is a mystery to life; even death and grieving have rewards I could never imagine.

Have you ever found yourself becoming very excited about attending a workshop by a famous teacher or reading a spiritual book that has gotten huge amounts of press? Perhaps that excitement lasted even after you finished the book or returned home from the workshop. Inevitably, though, the glow fades and you wonder what all the hype was about. You might even become angry or cynical, "Well, that sounded good, but it was just the same old thing." "What a lot of garbage; there's nothing here (in this book, in this teaching) that has any substance. It's all fluff. It's spiritual pabulum."

What happened? I am sure I have been duped by some sharp-talking, New Age version of a snake-oil salesman, but I think many other times I am attracted and drawn to someone else's experience of life in the Spirit. I am attracted to the truth of what they speak and what they have learned in the light of their experience. Here is the difficulty: these teachers are speaking to me from *their* experience of truth. I know it is the truth for me as well because it resonates in the heart of me, but in order to be able to attain that truth the way they have, I also must have the experience of it. No matter how skilled or holy the author might be, no one can give *their* experience to me.

Immediately after a workshop or class, we can get very high on the ideas and concepts presented to us. We can become all fired up to live differently or to create new healthy practices. When we come back down to our own limited perception of reality again, we think nothing has changed except now we are annoyed or angry about the money or the time we spent. We can only learn from our own experience, not from someone else's. As wonderful and awe inspiring as someone else's enlightenment experience might be, it will do nothing to make us enlightened. We forget this truth and in our forgetfulness become frustrated and disillusioned.

With letting go, as well as with most other things in life, it is the experience that teaches you, not the words.

With letting go, as well as with most other things in life, it is the experience that teaches you, not the words. Whatever workshops, books, or CDs are calling to you, know that you need to relate all these ideas to your own experiences and glean the necessary truths for yourself.

Buddha was once approached by a woman who had lost her son. She was devastated. She thought her grief was unbearable. She asked the Buddha how she could be relieved of this pain. Buddha told her to go into the village close by and collect a mustard seed from every household she encountered which had not experienced this kind of loss. She was asked to bring those seeds back to him and then he would give her a message of healing.

The woman hurried on her way, grieving still, but looking forward to a swift ending of her pain. She returned to the Buddha empty handed. Every household she visited had, at some time, experienced pain and loss as deep as her own. She looked at the Buddha with eyes both sad and wise, knowing his lesson to her was, "I cannot take away your pain. Be aware you are not alone, and know your pain is not only a reflection of your loss, but your love as well."

Hidden within our grieving, especially when it involves sickness or death, is the sense of our own mortality. We can focus on how much we will miss her and how sad we are that he is leaving us. That is true but, in many cases, it is our own death and transitory nature we are fearful of looking at or accepting. Any death puts us face to face with our own.

Aside from my initial recovery when I was fairly numb and unaware of my feelings, my most significant adult and conscious encounter with grieving came with the death of my mother. The loss of a family member is difficult enough, and when it is unexpected, it is even more difficult to deal with. Not only did my mother's death follow only three months after my father's death, but my mother was vibrant and in good health. She was looking forward to the rest of her life, and I was looking forward to enjoying it with her.

I was home in Louisville when my Mom's sister called me from Brooklyn with the news. I went upstairs stunned and more than a little lost. I kept hearing the words of an old Harry Chapin song in my head, "Would you put your light on please, it's kind of dark tonight…" over and over. I packed my bag and called for my ticket to New York.

I arranged most of the funeral myself, spoke her eulogy, and lead the prayers at the cemetery. I was quite choked up and ready to cry at times, but I stuffed the tears because I had something important to do for my mother and our family. I remember telling myself, "I will cry later."

Later never came. I left Brooklyn, returned to Louisville, and went back to my teaching job with a deep sadness and emptiness but no tears. I knew the tears were there, they just would not come to the surface. I even tried to force them out, and that is when I discovered that grieving comes when it will. The feelings will express themselves at their own good time, not one of my conscious choosing.

It was not until almost a year later that the tears came. Libby, a dear friend and colleague of mine had just been fired from her job. I had worked with her for a number of years, and she was tremendously influential in teaching me the ropes of counseling and working with clients. I was angry and sad about the unfairness of it all. I was mulling over all these feelings in the car on my way home from work, and then the grieving hit me. I had to pull over to the side of the road, and as I did I cried and sobbed more deeply than I could ever remember. I knew I was crying for my friend, and I became aware that the tears were also for my mother. Along with all of that I felt bits and pieces of all of the other losses in my life.

When I grieve, other grieving issues, even ones which are long past, come to consciousness. I also need to remember that I grieve in layers, not all at once.

I have counseled many people who have experienced working through a deep grief only to have it resurface. They have found themselves hurt and confused. People will then tend to discount their past work at grieving, and say something to the effect of, "Well, I must have been fooling myself. I really thought I was working through things, but I guess not." That kind of thinking is a trap. What is happening here is that our mind, our intellect, is attempting to interpret the feelings, but as happens so often, using the intellect to interpret feelings does not work terribly well. It is similar to using a screwdriver to hammer a nail. It can be done but not very effectively. The intellect looks at the feelings of grief we are having and says to itself something such as, "Oh, those feelings are very similar to (another grief issue)," and then pulls up all the past issues that have a similar flavor. It is easy to become overwhelmed by this information until we realize what is happening. The intellect is trying to categorize all these feelings of grief. It wants to label them and box them up. It is the mind's way of organizing and controlling. We just need to be aware that even though there is only the present grief to be dealt with, that the mind and emotions are open to recalling all of the other grieving we have experienced.

When you notice the mind attempting to overly rationalize your grief process you need to immediately get back to your truth which is: "My past work on grieving this issue is true and sound. I am now being asked to go deeper into my sadness, and I will continue to heal." A deep process of grieving is not completed with a single pass. Many times grieving requires working through the process on a deeper level. The human psyche has a way of giving us just what we can handle rather than handing us the whole package at once.

How do I know I have completed the process and arrived at surrender? Many people think the measure of completion is that I no longer have any feelings about the matter. Not true. I believe there will always be some residual sadness attached to major grieving issues, such as with a loved one who has passed on, but when grieving has reached the stage of surrender and acceptance, I will no longer feel myself being sucked into that black hole of pain. The sadness might be there, but I will have the power to embrace it, and the power to choose if I need to hold onto it longer or not. My job is to be at peace with whatever sadness might remain as I have honestly worked through my process of grief.

Looking back on a healed issue of grief would be like looking at a physical scar. I would remember the wound, the pain, yet I would not be really feeling it or reliving it. I can honor the wound, the hurt, and the loss and move on. I want to observe myself and notice that when I touch the area of life I have been grieving and surrendering that it no longer has a tremendous amount of energy to drag me in. Sadness is still here, yes, but it is no longer this black hole that overwhelms me. I can feel it and I can still be aware of all the other, even joyful, things in my life.

When I consider my emotional past, sometimes I see a litter-strewn highway or picture myself with this huge U-Haul cart I am dragging behind me filled with unfinished business. There are other times when my relationship with the past is kinder, nobler, and more gentle, but even the more benign reflection lets me know my past still needs cleaning up.

A child cries. That sound can always be gut-wrenching for me especially when it is happening in a big store that is loaded with stuff a kid would love. I know the child has seen something they feel they just must have. They are possessed by this gut-churning hunger that only this toy or that doll can fill. I remember as a child seeing a toy gun in a store window, along with many other things along the way, and having this huge yearning and emptiness inside of me. My mother asked me what was the matter and I told her I needed that toy. She, of course, told me I did not really need it, but she did not understand. I did not want it like she wanted a new hat or a pair of gloves. I needed it. I was consumed by that need.

There was a moment, a blessed moment, when my Mom really understood. It was a blustery fall day in Brooklyn. I was wearing one of my most prized possessions, a green felt cowboy hat with gold thread trim. I am not sure if I had my six-guns or not, but the hat itself was enough to fuel my fantasies of roaming the Old West even though we were in the middle of Ninth Street. A gust of wind took my hat off and blew it in the street where it rolled and tumbled into a noxious mixture of spittle and dog poop. As I went to get it, my mother grabbed me and said, "No. You are not going to touch that thing. It's filthy." I could understand her reasoning, but what was I going to do? I needed my hat. Then, before I could even raise an argument, we were on a bus going downtown to get a new cowboy hat. I couldn't believe it. She really got it.

If you approach a child with compassion rather than just reasonableness, you will be able to understand their hurt and pain, then you can help them move through it rather than dismissing it in an overly rationalistic way such as telling them, "There are much more important things in the world" or "Think about the starving kids in Korea." A lost bicycle for a seven year old might carry the same emotional weight as a repossessed car for an adult.

Children need to grieve just as adults do. I did not have any role models for grieving, so I wonder if other kids really know how to grieve, or if, like me, they stuffed the feeling and said to themselves, "OK, well I can't have it now but I will have it later." I wonder if these unexpressed and unrecognized grief issues from childhood are what might keep pulling us back to regressed states of mind and perception that make us lose touch with our adult self and react to life situations as a frightened and overwhelmed six year old. If we can help our children heal some of their wounds, I believe we can also heal ourselves.

Take the time to grieve your losses. Take some time to lovingly examine the things you did not get that have now become symbols of desire. Know them, embrace them. Understand that the hunger and the memories which are evoked are not about *things* so much as they are about deeper messages such as: "Listen to me; understand me; please do not make fun of my desires, respect them." Underlying many of the losses of our past is a deep yearning for wholeness and affirmation. We might never get that support from our parents and teachers, but as conscious beings we can become aware that we were not defective. We were not flawed, the methods of our teachers were. With that realization we can begin to open ourselves to the love and support and nurturing that is available to us.

I feel as if I have integrated and healed huge portions of my life, but in spite of all the things I know I "should" do, and all the things I should accept or surrender to, I continue to rebel at the apparent unfairness life seems to bring. I get angry, upset, bent out of shape when things don't work out the way I want them to, or the way I think they "should." There continues to live in me a defiant and sometimes childish part of my nature that wants to write all the rules, and expects the universe to start obeying them.

Here is another letting go and surrendering, embracing myself again, just where I am, not where I think I ought to be. I am the manifestation of an endless inventory of dichotomies and contradictions. I am sometimes wise, sometimes foolish, sometimes childish, sometimes grownup. I need to embrace it all.

There was once a holy monk who had many followers. At evening meditation, he was approached by a traveler who informed him that his teacher of many years had made his transition. The monk immediately got up and left for the funeral service of his teacher. When he arrived at the scene he began to cry, and his students were scandalized at what they perceived was a demonstration of emotion and attachment. "Master," a student asked, "why are you crying?" "Because I am sad," was the simple reply. That story and the briefest line in Christian scripture, "Jesus wept," (Jn 11:35) are confirmations enough for me of the necessity and the healthiness of grieving.

Since life is filled with comings and goings, birth and death, changes and transformations, when I am living life fully, I am in the middle of all of this. As difficult, painful, and paradoxical as all of these experiences can be, they can also be tremendously life-giving. I recall Ram Dass speaking of his work with dying AIDS patients. He described how he would feel deep love for the people he was working with and then realize he would be losing their physical presence very soon. He stated, "I am most alive when I am standing on the edge of love and heartbreak." I know what he is saying, but I am far from that level of openness and acceptance.

We do not need to focus on sadness or pessimism. We do need to enter life in the most passionate way, knowing there will be change, joy, loss, life, death, and resurrection. We will be touched with all these things and through it all we can know there is a deeper self, a consciousness that knows and is upheld by the changeless. In the words of the mystic philosopher Teilhard de Chardin, "It is your right and your duty to throw yourself into the things of the earth."

When I throw myself into the things of the earth, I will experience everything. I will not judge. I will learn I can love and grieve; I can be sad and joyous, and I can know the truth and beauty of it all. It is all learning. It is all grace. It is all good. It is all God.

Grieving is surrender. It is working through all the feelings that bring us to surrender. Grieving does not just lead to surrender, it leads to peace. It leads to the grace to open our hearts to life.

Life is change. Things are constantly shifting and so, in some ways, we are always grieving, letting go, making room. It is the way of things.

MEDITATION: RELEASING SADNESS

As you get comfortable, relaxed, and open,
take a few deep cleansing breaths, opening even more.

Count backwards from ten to one as you breathe deeply.
You can feel a sense of lightness and receptiveness as you allow Spirit
to speak to you, sharing with you exactly what you need.

Breathe deeply and experience yourself more and more relaxed as you
open to this meditation.

We are not dwelling on sadness. We are focused on healing.

As you allow yourself to relax, open to enhanced feelings of peace.

Breathe into that peacefulness. You may know it, feel it, sense it, or you
can simply imagine what it would feel like.

Let your mind go back to a piece of grieving you know you have already
worked through. Know that the memories are there, and perhaps even
some sadness remains as it usually does, but the memories no longer
grab you or pull you in. You can observe them as if you were looking into
a snow globe.

If you have not done so already, allow one finished memory of loss to
come into your consciousness, and as you observe it gently, notice all
the different feelings that were there.

If there was anger or sadness, notice those emotions were also a reflection of how deeply you cared about someone or something. Anger and
love–we do not usually think of them as similar, but you can realize you
are only angry about someone or something you feel deeply about.

The depth of your sadness is also the depth of your love.

If you have allowed yourself to learn from this experience, then you might even notice that some feelings have transformed. Your sadness can transform into compassion for another. Your anger can be better expressed as love.

Notice the differences for yourself.

There can be great learning in knowing that feelings and experiences can transform within us.

Let your sadness become compassion.

In gratitude, lovingly notice how you learn and how you grow.

Begin to be conscious again of your breathing. Breathe deeply and stretch. Come fully back here in your body, completely centered and grounded.

Get up, stretch, and look around you. Become familiar with the place again, feeling yourself in your body. Journal or process any other way you like.

NUGGETS

One of the ways of letting go of the baggage of my past is to grieve as consciously as I can all those losses I never gave myself a chance to feel.

We would not grieve if we did not love.

I think it is much too simplistic to dismiss our childhood losses as meaningless now that we are adults.

A major tenet of Buddhism reminds me all pain comes from being attached to something that is changeable. I believe that is true, but I also believe that to remove myself from my feelings removes me from my humanity as well.

I have counseled many people who had worked diligently on being conscious of their grieving and labored with insight and awareness through each stage as it became available. They were also aware of their surrender and acceptance and the relief and sense of unburdening that letting go gave them.

I understand how discouraging it can be when a thought, memory, or life experience triggers our grief and sadness all over again; I need to know it is usually not past grief but present grief I am experiencing.

One of my teachers related that when we are in the throes of grieving, it is as if we are viewing a photo album and are stuck on the last page. When we have reached through to acceptance, the whole album is available to us.

ADDICTIONS AND GRACE

(Addictions are multidimensional, having components that are physical, mental, emotional, and spiritual, and many have genetic components as well. The intent of this chapter is to focus on the spiritual side of addiction/attachment and the necessity of surrender.)

BECAUSE LIFE IS CHANGE, *we will all experience loss and need the surrender of grieving. Because most of us will first journey outside ourselves in our search for truth and wholeness, we will experience the spiritual lessons which come to us through our work with addictions and attachments. Hopefully, we will come to know the grace and power of surrender so that we might be free.*

Surrender saved my life. As with many other people caught up in the throes of a serious addiction, I was killing myself, and I did not know how to stop. There came a moment, unplanned and unforeseen, when all the facades of my ego collapsed. I could not deny my addiction and what it was doing to me any longer. I was the mountain climber letting go of the rope because I could do nothing else. At that moment of grace, I subtly became aware there was a power greater than my ego. I did not know to call it God since the power was so different from my old notions of God. This new found insight revealed a Higher Power, a power greater than my little self. It was a Power both intimate and transcendent, a part of me yet more than me.

The term addiction is generally used to describe compulsive drinking, drug using, gambling, smoking, as well as other obviously destructive behaviors. A word that is more Buddhist in nature is the term "attachment." Attachment carries both the Western connotation of the more serious forms of addiction as well as all those other behaviors and objects of desire that can drain us of life. An attachment is anything we cling to with the hope that it will bring us that which we desire. Paradoxically, as a result of our clinging, the attachment also becomes something that hinders us, holds us back, or makes us unhappy. Addictions and attachments are anything that distracts us from the truth, anything that contributes to us forgetting who we really are, and anything that gets in the way of our growth.

The human race is extremely eclectic when it comes to attachments. We can be attached to neatness or clutter; we can be attached to the characterization of victim or martyr; we can most certainly become addicted to chemicals such as nicotine, alcohol, cocaine, and many others. We can become addicted and attached to roles in life, attitudes, and beliefs. We can become attached to being right and even attached to our anger and our fears. In short, we can be addicted or attached to anything.

Whatever the name or whatever the form, addictions carry with them the false promises of the ego ...

Whatever the name or whatever the form, addictions carry with them the false promises of the ego which whispers as slyly as the serpent in the Garden of Eden, "Eat from me and I will give you life."

You can connect to the universal nature of addictions by exploring your answers to three simple questions: "Is there anything about yourself, or in your life, you would like to change?" "Do you have a fairly good sense of what is required to make those changes?" Some examples here would be: if you would like to get into better physical shape, you realize you need to change your eating habits and exercise more. If you desire to meditate more effectively, you realize it is necessary to create a time and a place to do that. Then the third question, the one that stumps everyone: "How come you are not doing it?"

The third question, "How come you are not doing it?" stops us in our tracks. The question raises to consciousness a sense of stuckness many of us might not be aware of. In struggling with the answer to that third question, we become conscious of our desire to change, but our inability to do so.

A classic example of attachment is illustrated in the Gospel story of the rich young man. He was already diligently working on his spiritual path, and he asked Jesus what more he could do. When Jesus told him to sell all his possessions and give the money to the poor and to follow in Jesus' path, scripture tells us that "he went away sadly because he had great possessions." (Mt 19:20-22)

Spiritual masters will tell us that it was not the riches that were the difficulty; it was the young man's attachment or addiction to his possessions that was the problem. We have often heard the Bible misquoted, stating, "Money is the root of all evil." The actual quote is, "The *love* of money is the root of all evil." (1 Ti 6:10)

The attachment or the addiction to money is what is holding him back. It is the love of money, not the money itself, which is creating the difficulty. The love of money makes it into an idol, a false god. Money becomes a means in itself. In this example, we make money the source of our abundance rather than God.

All of us have our addictions/attachments, and although some of them might be considered more debilitating than others, each one of us needs to decide for ourselves what is taking our energy, draining us of power, making us crazy, not allowing us to be the person we want to be, or hindering us from accomplishing what we would like.

When I was working in treatment, I would begin one of my talks by asking the group, "Why do you drink or use drugs?" Inevitably there would be a young person in the crowd who would eagerly wave his hand. The answer always would be, "To get high." Then I would ask, "Why did you want to get high?" No answer. It would be up to the rest of the group with more life experience to fill up all the chalkboards with answers to that question.

All of the answers fell into three categories. The first was wanting to stop feeling bad by getting rid of negative emotions such as guilt, fear and shame. The second was the need to feel good or better in order to celebrate, loosen up, be wittier and more sociable. The final reason was a desire to go beyond the normal, everyday view of life. This last reason for using was always difficult to put into words, but however the idea was expressed, it always suggested a sense of going beyond our usual way of perceiving the world and ourselves. People would use descriptions such as "getting out of myself," "wanting to touch the sky," and "searching for a sense of being a part of everything."

All the descriptions of the to-go-beyond category, as vague as they were, had a spiritual quality to them. These many descriptions also carried with them a sense of Oneness, what some refer to as unity consciousness. The Greek word "ecstasos" means "to get out of oneself," in the language of spirituality, to go beyond the confines of the ego, which was exactly the idea people were attempting to convey.

Wanting to feel good, not wanting to feel bad, and a desire to go beyond the bounds of the ego are all valid and very human desires. Addictive substances and behaviors seem to meet those desires for a time. The trap is either we never quite reach the desired state or it does not last long enough, so we go back to the substance or behavior again and again.

A character from Greek mythology presents a marvelous illustration of this never-ending downward spiral. Tantalus was condemned to Hades; his punishment was to be eternally hungry and thirsty. Just above his head was a bunch of grapes and right below his knees a stream of cool water. Every time he would raise up to eat the grapes they would move just beyond his reach, and each time he would stoop to drink the water, it would recede so low he could not reach it. This is a perfect picture for a person ensnared in addiction. There is nothing else to do but reach up or down, even though he already knows the results are fruitless.

Addictions are not bad or evil. They are a detour, an error, a mirage, a glamour in our thinking that convinces us they will take us where we want to go. Addictions offer us what seem to be an easy way to peace and wholeness but, in reality, they get in the way of Spirit.

How do we get so caught up in the "stickiness" of addictions and attachments? We begin our human existence as this wonderful integrated being, but very quickly our perception shifts. We enter into what a spiritual teacher refers to as "people training." People start telling us who we are. The most unfortunate part about that is, all the people who are telling us who we are don't know who they are!

Then we start getting other messages such as, "Don't do that." "You're a bad boy or a bad girl." We start becoming fearful and protective, and without even thinking about it very much we start wrapping ourselves around this fragile little ego-consciousness which can get all broken up over anything. As we protectively become more and more enmeshed in this little piece of ourselves we also start thinking that this is all that we are. Our perception of self becomes limited and trapped in our very restricted and frightened ego. We forget we are much more than our ego; we forget we are a unique expression of the Divine. That forgetting is reinforced all the time, at home, at school, and church. Over and over we learn that what we know and what we do is who we are. It takes years to begin to know we are so much more than that.

We are born perfect. We are born whole. We are born integrated. We are this wonderful combination of our spiritual nature, our soul, and also our human nature which is sometimes referred to as our ego. When we are still in our early, balanced state of perfection, our ego is like a little ship that goes out into the world to explore. It comes back and reports to the soul something like, "Oh, it is really OK out there." Then after a little while, the ego feels attacked by all this people training and all this focus on behavior. It becomes fixated on messages such as, "You are bad," and any other kind of label that gets stuck on us. The ego becomes very fearful and defensive, and because we identify with it so fully, we become fearful and defensive as well. It seems that everything in our young life contributes to this ego-identification. School focuses on our intellect, an instrument of the ego. Our home life is filled with messages focusing on behavior, and so we begin to think as the ego thinks, "I am what I do." Even in church we are told we are sinners. Instead of focusing our attention on our Spirit, we are forced to focus on what others are telling us is wrong with us.

In my early religious training, I learned very quickly that I had an immortal soul that was just absolutely wonderful. My soul was made in the image and likeness of God; it was eternal. My soul would live forever, but the downside was my soul never seemed to do anything. When the rest of me decided to do something bad, my soul just seemed to wimp out. Here is this marvelous and eternal part of me, made in the image and likeness of God and it doesn't do anything! All the drive I was experiencing in my life was coming from my ego.

My body, my mind, and my emotions wanted what they wanted and they went ahead and did what they wanted to do, and my soul sounded like an old Mr. Bill movie, always somewhat aghast, exclaiming, "Oh no!" It would whine but not much else. It did not seem to have any power. I thought there was something wrong with that picture, but I could not figure out what it was or how to change it. No one ever taught me about the power of the soul and what the soul did or how it worked, because they did not know about it themselves.

As we are growing up, our identification with the ego is continually reinforced whenever we experience ourselves as not being enough. Nobody has to tell you that in words, you just kind of "get it" from what other people say and do. A look of disappointment from a parent or teacher conveys the message loudly and clearly, "You are not enough." The ego holds onto that message as an ultimate truth.

Along with the ego being "not-enough," it is also paradoxically the epitome of self-centeredness. The ego is that part of me that says, "I want what I want, and I want it right now. I don't care what *you* want; this is what I want." It is not that nobody else exists, the ego just does not care. My ego also has the mentality of a three year old. It has not grown much over the years, and I do not expect it to.

The ego is not an awful thing, it is just a very limited thing. When I am looking at myself through the eyes of my ego, I am looking at myself in a very limited way. When I perceive the world through the eyes of my ego it is very difficult to look beyond the tip of my nose. Living from ego-consciousness is a constricted and painful existence. It is only natural to look for some relief.

The first place we go seeking relief is inside ourselves, but then we remember, "I'm not enough," so there is no sense looking inside. Then I look outside, and guess what I see? It is wonderland. It is a smorgasbord. Everyone and everything is telling me, "Do this. Do that. Eat me. Drink me. I will make you feel better." If we turn on the TV we will notice our whole society is based on the concept of making us feel rotten so we buy something to make us feel better. There are billions of things out there that we can become attached to. I can become involved in what I am calling the more serious addictions or some of the more subtle ones such as power, control, being a victim or a martyr. I can even become addicted to all the many forms of distorted thinking about money, or scarcity, or anger, or guilt, or shame.

The appealing part of addictions is they give us a taste of what we are after. We discover this thing (drugs, alcohol, money, gambling, and sex) and we do it, and then exclaim, like so many others, "Oh, I found it! I found what I was looking for. I found the secret of life. All I have to do is have money, or drink a little, or gamble, or eat Twinkies, and I will be OK."

After one of my first encounters with alcohol, I thought to myself, "All I have to do now is mix a little alcohol with my life and I will be able to do everything I have ever wanted to do, and I will be able to do it well and without fear or anxiety." Of course it did not work that way, but notice how potent a thought that is and how powerful an attachment.

After a time with our substance or behavior of choice, we discover that it isn't working anymore and we find ourselves experiencing more pain than before. We continue to have all those old feelings of not being enough and something being wrong with us, and we also feel trapped in an addiction that is now causing much more pain than it is relieving.

This is the point of breakdown of the ego and it feels awful. It feels like the world is going to end, and there is some truth to that feeling. The world is going to end, but not in the way we think. It is also the moment of surrender and transformation. This, sometimes, is the most blessed moment we can experience, as painful as it might be.

In recovery literature, surrender is described as the ego reaching a stage of "calamity and collapse." The first three steps of recovery are often abbreviated as, "I can't do it. God can. I think I will let go and let God."

Surrender is not giving up. It is the opening of ourselves to transformation. Surrender is moving from a cramped position of being trapped, to an expansive place of freedom. Surrender takes place in my heart, not my head. I do not make it happen, I let it happen. The conscious work I need to do is to keep myself open to when and where surrender is more likely to happen. I can do that by cultivating a desire to change, through prayer, by working on my faith, and by reminding myself I am not alone. I am never going to know when all those actions are going to kick in and manifest in the material world, but grace is always happening.

A number of years ago, after I had done some more serious work on other major addictions in my life including my family-of-origin issues, I knew smoking was next. I already had the tools, and so I prayed and did all the things I knew how to do but nothing seemed to be happening. I was either buying cigarettes or bumming cigarettes, and still smoking.

All during this smoking time, from the moment I decided to quit, I was praying, and I was working on believing God can help me. I was working on knowing that God could help me and would help me. I was believing and working on all that and nothing seemed to be working.

Even though I was still smoking, one day I received a powerful insight in prayer. The insight was this, "Gerry, you are in the process of quitting smoking. Even though the process has not manifested in the material world yet; it will manifest. Do not give up on your efforts."

Fairly soon after that, I got up one day and I did not smoke. I don't even know when it was. I did not smoke the next day or the next. Even though I did not know I had quit, what was more important to me was that, at that moment, I realized I was working with God. I am very grateful that it has been over fifteen years, one day at a time, without a cigarette.

Here is a lesson: Grace is happening even when I do not know it. If I am dedicated to working on an aspect of my life and hold a positive intention in my heart, then I am loved and guided by Spirit even if I am not experiencing an outer manifestation of release or surrender. There are times when the moment of surrender is much more sudden and obvious, and that can be frightening. When I come to the moment of surrender, what happens is my ego blinks out of the picture for a second, and the reality of who I truly am comes shining through. "Wow," I realize, "that is who I am. I am that Light, that Love, and that Power. That is what God created me as. I'm not this crazy little ego that is running around like a decapitated chicken babbling, 'I want what I want, when I want it, and I want it right now.' I am not this insane, limited little piece that is getting addicted and attached to everything."

In surrender most of us do not know what is at the other end of letting go. We can be very afraid of surrendering into God because the God that shows up might be the God we learned about in school that is going to say "Gotcha," or "I've been waiting for you to let go." We might fear the old image of God, the God of judgment and recrimination is waiting for us, ready with some form of punishment. Like the mountain climber, at the moment of surrender, we might be tempted to ask, "Is there anybody else up there?"

What I discovered, and continue to discover, is that the God at the other end of surrender is beyond our wildest positive expectations. It is the God of unconditional love. It is the God of wisdom, power, strength, light, and peace. It is a God beyond what I could ever think or believe. Surrender into God is initiated by grace and is a grace in itself. In surrender I come to the realization of the unconditional love within me. Surrender opens me to the vision of who I really am. I realize that even through all of my addictive behavior, the truth has always resided inside of me.

Grace, which is the movement of God's Love and healing in my soul, can sometimes come to me very gently and subtly, as well as dramatically. Even in the most painful of times, grace is continually revealing to me a power greater than my ego. The Jungian analyst Marianne Woodman said it so beautifully, "God comes through the wound." Because that is true, in a very real way, addictions *are* grace. The realization of my addiction, or my attachment, can be a wakeup call to delve deeper into the reality of who I am, and a continuing challenge to find my way home. The grace of surrender manifests as a vision of me becoming a true and honest reflection of God's Love and Peace.

The gift of grace is that through our woundedness comes the Light of the world, the power and the presence of wholeness and peace. Once we experience the power of God through surrender, life will never be the same. Grace says, "Don't hide your light under a basket." Grace says, "Shine! You are the light and peace of the world; you are the love of God. Let your light shine and know that nothing, absolutely nothing, not sugar, or alcohol, or gambling, or debt, or the past, or food, or nicotine, nothing can really get in the way of that light and love and grace and peace that you are. You are the light and grace and peace of the world. Amen."

MEDITATION: ADDICTIONS

As you get comfortable, relaxed, and open, take a few deep cleansing breaths, opening even more.

Count backwards from ten to one as you breathe deeply. You can feel a sense of lightness and receptiveness as you allow Spirit to speak to you, sharing with you exactly what you need.

Breathe deeply and experience yourself more and more relaxed as you open to this meditation.

What are you holding onto—or is there something in your life that seems as if it is holding onto you?

Our addictions and attachments take many forms, and we all have a truckload of them. Know that as we learn and grow we become more aware of what is holding us back. We not only become more aware of our attachments, we also become more aware of their false promises, and so it becomes a little easier to release and let go.

As you relax, allow to come to mind a thing or an emotion or habit or behavior that is controlling you more than you are controlling it. Just let it come to you. It might not be what is uppermost on your mind. You might even be surprised at what surfaces. That's all right, just let it come to you.

Breathe.

Again, take a moment to examine it. This is not judgment, you are simply becoming more aware of this behavior or emotion and what it is you are trying to gain from it.

You are probably going to see you are not getting what you want, that this behavior or emotion is not giving you what it might have promised.

Take that addiction or attachment and hold it gently in your hands and allow your prayer to be:

"God, I have forgotten that You are the source of my strength, love, wisdom, peace, and abundance.

I let go of this behavior or feeling into Your loving hands and open myself to receiving from You, my Source, that which I truly need and desire.

Thank you, God."

Be open. Know that the seed has been planted. You can nurture it consciously whenever you think of it and you can know that it is growing even when you are not thinking of it.

Begin to be conscious again of your breathing. Breathe deeply and stretch. Come fully back here in your body, completely centered and grounded.

Get up, stretch, and look around you. Become familiar with the place again, feeling yourself in your body. Journal or process any other way you like.

NUGGETS

Some people would rather die than change their minds.

Our primary wound is our sense of separation from God.

Do you remember when you were whole?

My addiction is not who I am. In fact, my addiction is a denial of who I am.

For many of us, addictions and attachments are part of the spiritual journey. In a very real way addictions are grace; they are a wakeup call to realize that we are much more than our egos. Addictions are the way we find our way home.

When it comes to addictions, I get "hooked" more than just once.

There are some traditions that would say that the ego is just part of our imagination, that it is not real. However, whether the ego is real or not, we are going to have to contend with it most of our lives.

Most of the world is constructed in such a way as to push us to seek outwardly what we can only find within ourselves.

The Latin word for "baggage" is *impedimenta*. What a great description for an addiction/attachment. Attachments get in the way of my growth, they get in the way of how I perceive myself, they get in the way of my relationship with other people, with God, and my own spiritual nature.

Addictions and attachments may be unnecessary, but as long as we have skin, they will be part of our lives.

In this topsy-turvy world we grew up in, the part of ourselves that is not supposed to be all that important, the ego, is running the whole show.

As long as we are living out of our limited ego-consciousness, those messages of "not enough" and "something wrong" will motivate most of our thoughts and actions.

Have you ever looked into a little baby's eyes? What you see there is absolute integration and wholeness. The little baby is not conscious of that perfection or wholeness, but it is there. One of the goals you have in life, if not *the* goal, is to reach a state where you are consciously aware of that perfection and integration. Your goal is to be perfectly and consciously aware of your Godliness.

Jesus did that; He became perfectly aware of His Oneness with God. Becoming Christ means to become aware of my Oneness with God. Being Christ, becoming the Anointed One, is becoming aware of the perfection and the God nature that is inside of me and letting that light shine.

IT JUST DOESN'T MATTER

HERE I SIT, *like a store clerk, with a labeler in my hand, putting stickers and price tags on all of the many things in my life. It is a very understandable human practice. Yet I also need to remember what is truly important, what is unchangeable. When I do, I find my clinging will fade. When I surrender my attachment to something, I do not necessarily need to give up the thing itself. I let go of the clinging, the holding on, and I let go of the static meaning I have put on it. I call to mind the words of Jesus, "Store up riches for your-selves in heaven where moths and rust cannot destroy." (Mt 6:20)*

Anytime I cling or become overly attached to something or someone, it means I am attached to who and what they are now. I do not always realize or accept the fact that what I am clinging to is already gone. My "new" car is no longer new, my new sleek slim body after liposuction is starting to sag and show bulges, the perfect person I fell in love with is becoming all too human. All that exists in this material universe, even relationships, will change and shift and, yes, come to an end.

Bill Murray was in a summer camp movie called *Meatballs*. He was playing one of his paradoxical wise-out-of-control-compassionate characters. One of the highlights of the summer was that Murray's camp would have a competition with the camp across the lake. The across-the-lake camp was made up of kids with a lot of money, who had all the advantages such as good equipment, coaches, training, and well-groomed practice fields. Murray's camp was made up of middle-class kids; the cabins, food, and equipment were adequate, but nothing special.

Inevitably Murray's camp would get their butts whipped by the kids across the lake, but every year, like Charlie Brown with the football, they would come back with dreams and hopes of getting on top.

The first day of the "Olympics" was a disaster, as in years past. As Murray was driving the bus home, he saw how down and dejected the kids were, and he started in on one of his seemingly nonsensical but extremely loud monologues. At the end of his tirade, he said "...and you know, if we win or lose this 'Olympics,' who cares? What difference will it make, tomorrow or five years from now? Is it going to get you a good job? Is it going to guarantee a college education? Is it going to set you up for life?"

"You wanna know what this whole thing is all about? Well, it just doesn't matter!" He said it again, "IT JUST DOESN'T MATTER!" It became a chant, and all the kids on the bus picked it up, and all the kids at camp picked it up, and began pounding their feet and clapping their hands, chanting, "It just doesn't matter; it just doesn't matter!" They were going wild; it was a wonderful, freeing moment.

That scene got me to thinking. How often in life do I put a value on something that is not real, not necessary, or not even my value to begin with?

You might want to try this if you are having a difficult day. Every once in awhile during the day, especially when you feel stressed out, stop for a moment, take a deep breath, and say to yourself, "It just doesn't matter." Try it again, "It just doesn't matter!" Again, louder this time, "IT JUST DOESN'T MATTER!" If it is feasible to say it out loud, perhaps in the privacy of your car, do it, yell it, "It just doesn't matter!"

You can learn quite a bit from that little exercise. Could you say it at all? Why not? If you did say it, was it freeing? Were you able to look at or think about that situation differently? Many times the circumstances do not change, but the way we perceive them does–and that makes all the difference.

This is not a suggestion that you quit your job or leave your family or let all the dishes pile up. Take the kids in Murray's camp: they still pursued their goal of winning the "Olympics" but did so now with a sense of fun, joy, and non-attachment as they realized the world and the rest of their lives did not hinge on the results, and that they were more important than the event itself.

Some life situations will continue to matter, but many others will wither when we confront them with the *Meatball's* chant, "It just doesn't matter."

If a family member becomes ill, a financial crisis occurs, or a serious accident happens, all of a sudden the many other things that I was so concerned about become petty and insignificant. I still need to take care of them, but they no longer carry the weight they had before. They matter, but compared to other more important things in my life, their importance is greatly diminished. As we grow in spiritual awareness we begin to realize the difference between the values our ego is attached to and those which are truly important.

We begin to discover the ego-things that grab us, make us self-centered, a little crazy and difficult to deal with. If we pay attention to our ego's attachments, we begin to realize that some values we have held to be almost sacred are, in reality, meaningless.

A classic example of a totally pointless worldly value is "being right." It is the cause of most wars, arguments, and other uncomfortable human encounters. We spend hours, days, even lifetimes proving ourselves to be right, and to what advantage? What do we get even if we are right? What does it matter?

Back in my high school teaching days I was a debate coach. My kids, who were all quite good at what they did, would march into a room with boxes of notes, index cards, magazines, books, and all sorts of other myriad references and proofs for whatever arguments they might need. Each year every high school in the nation would be given the same topic to debate. Everyone would practice being an expert on either side of the argument. It just didn't matter who was right or not. What mattered was how good you were at arguing your point, how much research you did, how many proofs you dug up for your arguments.

My son-in-law John is from the southern part of Ireland. He was telling me about a gentleman he worked for years ago from the north of Ireland, which historically has been allied with England. One of John's favorite subjects is history and one day during a lunch break the Northerner suggested that John pull a history book off the bookshelf and thumb through it. John was amazed. He related that he recognized the dates for most of the historical events, but the description of the events was totally different from the way he had learned them. What John might have learned as a sneak attack or horrible injustice was looked upon by the other side as an act of self-defense or a triumph of justice. It is true, the winners write the history from their own point of view, or in this case each side had their own interpretation of the same event.

"I know I'm right, and I'll show you." I might look it up in the almanac or encyclopedia. I have known people to get into physical fights over something each thought was right; the winner of the fight, of course, was right, even if he was wrong. Human beings have extended this same concept into a larger scale—it is called war.

Suppose for a moment that I am having a heated discussion with you about what happened last Saturday. I am convinced I am right, and you are convinced you are right. Let us suppose by the strength of my argument, I prove to you that I am right, and therefore, you are wrong. What have I gained? I have a brief moment of ego exaltation, and a moment of puffed-up superiority, which I do not deny certainly does feel good, but after that, what?

Just what have I gotten out of being right? What has my "being right" done to our relationship?

When I am aware of my ego's need to be right I also become aware there are ideas, attitudes, beliefs in my life which really are clutter. They are just stuff, things that I thought mattered but really do not, and it requires vigilance, looking, searching, honesty, and practice to be able to let these things go.

There are times when we become so focused on one area of our lives we miss everything else. Sometimes that is a good thing when a task deserves all of our attention. Too often, however, our attachment becomes so intense our vision becomes distorted. Something has started to matter so much that we can't see straight. The Oriental poem called *The Archer* describes the bowman as having perfect vision and aim when he is simply shooting arrows at the target, but when a prize is offered, his hands begin to shake and his vision becomes blurry. His proficiency is still there, but his attachment to the prize has begun to blind him, and pull him away from his talent. Does the prize matter? Of course it does, but when we become attached to it, we lose our focus. We lose our talent. We lose our ability to know what is most important.

There are many times when clients of mine will experience themselves as overwhelmed with the conditions of their lives. Along with many other circumstances, they will talk to me about depression, lack of self-love, or the impossibility of life in general. Then it is up to me as an observer to ask them, "How do you know this? Can the overwhelmed part of you know it is overwhelmed, or does that knowing have to come from another aspect of yourself?"

It is fascinating to me that a day or a few hours before a person comes to a therapy session, they enter into this Observer consciousness. They review the past week or weeks of their lives and become aware of what worked and what did not. They observe their emotional states without being overly involved in them. They do this so unconsciously, they do not realize they are cultivating this most important tool for awareness and healing.

"How do you know you are depressed?" you might ask yourself. "How do you know you are overwhelmed? How do you know your life is out of control?"

When people are willing to ask those questions, they begin to realize there is an aspect of the self that is outside the box. There is a part of the self that is not involved with the depression, the fear, or of being out of control. The person can become aware that he is experiencing depression, being overwhelmed, or feeling out of control, but that is not all that he is. There is a part or aspect of the self that is outside that experience.

As suggested previously, it is the essence of many spiritual paths to cultivate this objective, Observer awareness. The witness or Observer is at the heart of detachment. Far from pathological disassociation, when I am in Observer consciousness I am very much in touch with all my feelings and emotions. I may continue to be affected by them, but I am no longer identified with them. Choice opens up when I am not attached. Not only am I able to put the circumstances of my life in perspective, I am able to make healthy choices about handling them.

There is a marvelous control button on some computer programs called "zoom out." When you press this button, all of a sudden you can see a much broader picture. It usually looks quite different from the little piece you might have been working on. The only way you can see clearly is by taking a step back, to zoom out for a moment. The larger picture gives perspective, and many times that perspective may change your ideas, opinions, attitude, and actions.

There are many examples for all of us that point out life's lessons only after the fact, or only after we can get a more complete view of the subject. When we are "in it" we don't really know what the situation means or how it is affecting us.

While I was in the middle of struggling with an addiction, and becoming aware of the damage it was doing in all areas of my life, there was nothing of value I perceived in it. Today, however, I look at my experience with addiction as being one of my greatest gifts. It taught me, as perhaps nothing else could, the meaning of surrender. My recovery helped me to be open to a world of Spirit, love, growth, and self-acceptance I never knew existed. There have been many times when I have thought to myself, "If I had never started down that path of addiction, I never would be experiencing the blessings of recovery, and I might just be the most miserable little person you ever met."

My Observer also makes me aware that values change. What matters to me will change. What grabs me today might not grab me tomorrow. I can walk by a store and something will catch my eye, something I did not even know existed a few seconds ago, and before I know it, it has me. I am hooked. I am already devising ways to make it mine. I have already been drawn into the game of "I-won't-be-happy-unless-I-have-it." That is so wild. This material object, I did not even know existed a few seconds ago has now taken a major place in my value system. What a world; what a wonder it is to be human! Here I am thinking I am on this wonderful spiritual path of goodness and light and, in an instant, I am being held captive by a new flash for my camera that has features I will probably never use or even be able to figure out. Although the attachment and longing are powerful, I need to ask myself, "How much does this really matter?"

Even today I wonder about the things I put value on. I see something in a store or the paper and I just have to have it. I think about my job, and how I just have to have this office or that position. Then I think of all the things I just had to have a few yesterdays ago. Most of them I did not get, and so what? Most are such a distant memory, they are virtually forgotten.

What made me forget? Probably something else came to mind that I had to have that replaced the former desire, and it too has died away over the years only to be replaced by other things I become obsessed about, addicted to, or attached to. Today it is a camera, a remodeled kitchen, a new chair, an angry thought, something I have to be right about, the ring I saw in a magazine, or that new book that is going to change my life. What will it be tomorrow?

What is truly important here; what really matters?

Not only do my values change with time, but they also change with circumstances. If I am walking down the street and I am hungry, what am I going to notice the most? Places to eat, right? It does not mean there are no jewelry stores or book stores or clothing shops on the block, it is just that I am not paying attention to them. At the moment those other places do not matter to me. Food places do matter.

If it were raining one day, and I was walking down the same street, and had a hole in my shoe, I might totally disregard the restaurants and fast food places, and be looking for a shoe store or shoe repair place, or some other place to help me with my problem. Again, it is not that the other stores do not exist; they are just not important to me at the moment.

There are also times when I do not know intellectually what something means, but I intuitively know it is important. The lessons about values and what matters continue as we discover life situations which force us to go deeper than our reason or intellect can take us. We move into what in Buddhism is called the "Don't Know Mind." When we become willing to let go of all our labels, all our limiting intellectual compartments of meaning, we can become freer and less encumbered. By surrendering the supremacy of intellectual understanding, we open ourselves to deeper meaning and purpose.

Not knowing does not mean not caring or walking in naive oblivion. It simply means that at this moment, I do not know what my experience means. I *think* I know what it means, but I do not know. I will let go of my supposed meaning and continue to pray for guidance to do what I need to do. I let go of my limited understanding and allow myself to be open to deeper knowing. I become less attached to my own meaning of things. I accept that I do not see the whole picture, and do not need to judge an event until it is over or until I have fully experienced it.

A few years ago I felt an urgent call to travel to South Dakota. I had been asked by a Jesuit priest in charge of a mission out there to work with both the Native Americans and the staff regarding alcohol, drug, and codependency issues. At the time I had a pleasant home, good job, and was a well-known and contributing member of the community. To all external purposes a move of those dimensions did not make sense. To be honest, it did not make sense to me either, but I knew it was something I had to do. While I was there, I thoroughly enjoyed my work and the people I was with, made a lot of mistakes, and learned much more than I had bargained for. I eventually called this my "desert experience," because it brought me in touch with some major issues in my life I had been avoiding either consciously or unconsciously. I thought I knew what my decision was all about. In reality, I did not have a clue. It was not until the experience was over that I began to discover what its meaning was for me.

Letting go of my limited understanding of a situation and being more in the flow of life is illustrated beautifully in a story from the Oriental tradition.

There was an old farmer who lived with his son. They were poor, but owned a wonderful black stallion. It was a magnificent beast and the pride of the old man and his son. One day the horse ran away. The neighbors heard about the tragedy and came to console the old man. "Oh," they said, "what bad luck, your horse ran away. We know you are poor, now you are even poorer because your prized possession is lost." The old man looked at them solemnly and said simply, "Good luck, bad luck, who knows?" Well, the next day, the stallion returned bringing with him fifteen wild mares, and he led them right into the corral. The neighbors heard of this and came to congratulate the farmer on his wonderful fortune. Again he replied, "Good luck, bad luck, who knows?"

As the old man and his son began to break and train the mares in order to take them to market, the son was thrown by one of the horses and broke his leg. Again, the neighbors streamed back, somewhat reminiscent of Job's neighbors, and commiserated with the farmer that his one helper, his only son was now incapacitated. What bad luck! Again the farmer replied, "Good luck, bad luck, who knows?"

It seems the country was getting ready to enter a very destructive war. The country was small, had few resources, and the enemy was much stronger and more powerful. Many of the country's young people would die. And so it was that the army began marching through the countryside conscripting all the eligible young men, but of course the farmer's son could not go because his leg was broken. The neighbors came and told the farmer how lucky he was. The farmer replied...Yes, you can guess what.

As we grow, we can also realize many of our values came from other people such as parents, clergy, and teachers. We adopted those values ourselves because they seemed right at the time, and they became so much of the fabric of our lives that we never questioned them. They have simply become our values.

It is a challenge to examine values and determine what are mine and what I have taken on from someone else. I can be unknowingly influenced by the importance other people put on certain material objects, a particular career, or set of religious beliefs. People can follow someone else's path unconsciously and end up with lives that are devoid of meaning even though their outside accomplishments might have been significant. Living a lifetime from values not our own is such a waste. The words of Thoreau come to mind, "Oh God, to have reached the point of death and to find that I have never really lived."

I need to be sensitive to the values of others, but I also need to be clear about the boundary between their values and mine. In the midst of examining my own values and what I hold as being important, it is always a revelation (and sometimes an unpleasant surprise) when I discover a value or belief that I held dear and important was not really mine at all. For instance, the love of professional success might have been my father's. Because he held it as important, I thought it needed to be important to me, and so I might have developed a strong drive for achievement. As a child I am like a little sponge. I can absorb the values of others so thoroughly I truly think they are mine. With success, for example, I pursue it thinking it is important to me, and then I when I get what I have been after, a high-paying prestigious job, or a Ph.D., or whatever it might be, I might find my accomplishment empty and void of meaning. I may think, "This is not enough; I need to achieve more." Then I spend my entire life doing just that. The process never ends. I am never happy or satisfied.

It requires honest and willing introspective work to determine what is important to you, and the difference between your values and those of others.

I am the one who gives events and life circumstances meaning.

I decide, and the meaning I assign things is greatly dependent on my perception, how I see it, what context I see it in. The meaning I put on things flows from my perception. Limited perception results in limited meaning.

We can surrender and let go of the meaning we put on the events of life in order to go beyond the intellect's limited understanding. We can accept that right now we only see imperfectly or, as in Plato's "Allegory of the Cave," we see only shadows and think they are the real thing.

We not only assign meaning to life circumstances; we also decide what matters and what does not.

"It just doesn't matter" doesn't mean our feelings are unimportant. We are not denying feelings, just detaching from them. "It just doesn't matter" means it will pass, and in the larger picture, even if we have a zoom-out button, we will only know a piece of life's puzzle. "It just doesn't matter" means giving up the illusion that I know, that I understand.

It is healthy for me to question my values from time to time. It is a good idea to take time out and look at my motives, my wants, and even my needs, to notice if they match up with who I am today. I can be quite surprised when they do not.

I am not suggesting we simply say nothing is really important and take all our clothes off and jump into the ocean. I am suggesting that the deeper and more honestly we are willing to look at the stuff of our lives, we will shed ourselves of much unneeded baggage with the realization that "It just doesn't matter."

We will continue to realize the value of an object, or even an experience, does not usually lie within its intrinsic nature but is an arbitrary value we put on it for any number of reasons. It is important to me because: I like it; someone I love likes it; it belonged to my Aunt Frances; I feel bad or I miss it when I don't have it (like Linus' blanket); it makes me feel safe; or a myriad of other reasons.

It just doesn't matter, it just doesn't matter. The bathroom still needs cleaning, the taxes need to get done… and in the midst of our daily lives can we gently touch what *really* matters? Who needs to be loved now? Where is the love in this situation and how can I show it? What is my lesson? What is my growing edge? Where is God in this?

Are you seeing the larger picture?

Will this be important tomorrow?

Is this your value or someone else's?

Is it your value now?

Is it a true need or an attachment?

It just doesn't matter. Does it matter? How important is it?

Only you can answer.

MEDITATION: IT JUST DOESN'T MATTER

(This is an exercise that you can choose to do anytime during the day without making it into a formal meditation.)

As you get comfortable, relaxed, and open, take a few deep cleansing breaths, opening even more.

Count backwards from ten to one as you breathe deeply. You can feel a sense of lightness and receptiveness as you allow Spirit to speak to you, sharing with you exactly what you need.

Breathe deeply and experience yourself more and more relaxed as you open to this meditation.

Imagine that auditorium full of kids stomping their feet, clapping their hands, and chanting: "It just doesn't matter; it just doesn't matter!"

What were you worried about last week? What were you worried about a year ago?

Relax and let whatever it is come to you. What is it that you can hold differently right now? What is something that mattered a short time ago that either doesn't matter as much or doesn't matter at all?

Just let that come to you, whatever it is.

Pause…Breathe…

As you hold it, notice what changed.

What did you let go of? What healed?

Be aware of how quickly ideas and concerns come and go in the mind. The mind always needs something to chew on.

Since you are the thinker of your thoughts, you can always let go.

Begin to be conscious again of your breathing. Breathe deeply and stretch. Come fully back here in your body, completely centered and grounded.

Get up, stretch, and look around you. Become familiar with the place again, feeling yourself in your body. Journal or process any other way you like.

NUGGETS

Surrender is not simply a principle applied to emotional and spiritual situations, it is also an important practice in the physical world. There are times when I just need to let go!

Perhaps when I reach enlightenment I will have a total "zoom-out" button that will let me see the whole picture. Until then I need to be satisfied with only partial images. Even when I am "zoomed out" and as objective as I can be, I know my ability to perceive the whole picture is still quite limited.

There is a tremendous freedom in not knowing, in not having to know.

What really matters and what doesn't? Have you ever been able to realize "It just doesn't matter" about something you really thought did matter, or mattered in the past?

When something matters to me I am putting a meaning and a value on it. I want to be aware that this meaning I have come up with is just a label. It is a marker to help me realize what this is at this moment in my life. It would be helpful to me to know that the meaning and value might change–it probably will. As my meaning of a thing changes so does its importance. Values I might have today might be unimportant tomorrow.

The need to be right still grabs me more often than I would like to admit. I remember a workshop participant once asking me, "Has anyone ever asked you a question you did not have an answer for?" Well, that was one I could not answer!

When I think my opinion is being questioned, even when someone asks me to repeat what I might have said, I find myself insulted and defensive. Now that's ego! Indeed the idea, "I'd rather be right than happy," comes back to haunt me all too often.

Once in a while it is helpful to ask, "Whose values are these?"

I can honor and respect your values without taking them on myself.

Only you can decide what really matters to you, but you also decide what *doesn't* matter. You can also sort out the clutter, the "stuff," of your life that you can do without.

In putting all things in perspective I bring to mind the wonderful declaration by Augustine, "You have made our hearts restless and they will never rest until they rest in Thee."

WHO DO YOU THINK YOU ARE?

"I'M A DOCTOR." "I'm a mother." "I'm a homeowner." "I'm a Catholic." "I'm a liberal." "I'm a Republican." "I'm a man." "I'm a ..." All the roles we have in life might be important, but none of them are who you are. As significant as the roles you play in life are, they are not who *you are. There can be no labels if you are to be free.*

Imagine a closet filled with all sorts of different costumes. There is an outfit for play, for work, for being a mom or dad, for being a son, daughter, brother or sister, just to name a few. Often there is more than one uniform for a particular role. In the play section of the closet, for example, there might be separate clothes for the role of photographer, tennis player, or musician. Depending on time and circumstances, you pick the suitable dress for the occasion.

No matter what outfit you choose and no matter what the reasons behind your choice, there is always a "you" that is doing the choosing.

You are not your uniform. Your attire simply serves you in a particular role or task you are performing. It helps you focus your energies in a certain way, and allows other people to have a sense of your role at a particular moment. Your role and your uniform have importance, but they are not who you are.

There are significant roles I act out in life, and my life would be pretty dull without them. My spiritual truth tells me, "As important as your roles in life might be, they are not who you are." My roles of husband, grandfather, and minister define much of what I do. My more minor roles of musician, photographer, and writer also give a clue as to what I hold important, but they are not who I am either.

Think of how easy it is to identify with your role at a particular moment, and then remind yourself of how ridiculous it is to think that is all you are.

You have just finished your grocery shopping, and you are in the checkout line. Is that who you are, someone waiting in line? Of course not, but that is how you might define yourself at that moment. When your emotional self gets caught up in the drama of life, you can find yourself hindered and even trapped by your role. You become somebody stuck in traffic, somebody who is outraged, or somebody who is busy. You lose touch with who you are.

I can become attached to any identity or role, and similar to many other attachments, I think my attachment keeps me safe. I am safe within the walls of my well-defined role. When I identify with being the boss, the mom, the guy who sweeps the streets, then I think I know who I am.

Life in the Spirit calls for us to delve more deeply into knowing who we are. We need to go deeper than our worldly identities and roles in life. We might have a vague notion that we are more than these external definitions, but until we are living from our souls, we will never know our true identity.

As long as we are unaware of how easily we become attached to our roles in life, much of our time is spent acting out of our ego, our little false constricted self. How do we know that? Just watch the news. It is all ego and fear. We might know we are one with Spirit, but if we really were acting out of our true being the world would be a different place. Most of us are not connecting with or acting out of our Being, our true nature. We are missing the mark; we are asleep, and it is very easy to fall asleep.

I notice this falling-asleep phenomenon quite often. I could be in this great high spiritual place, and then something happens, and BAM, I find myself in fear and scarcity again. I become a victim of those fear-based feelings, and then I experience myself as isolated and separate from God, my source.

The pettiest of things can knock me out of serenity, and I will find myself moving from an experience of my true Self into my stuck little ego. I lose my keys; I have a flat tire. It could be a broken shoelace, a spilled cup of coffee, a forgotten appointment, an unexpected bill, a look, a remark, somebody slow in the checkout line, and I feel my identity imploding into this frightened little knot. The triggering thought could even be as far away from reality as what I think someone else might be thinking of me. I can physically feel this tightness and contraction. I experience my heart closing, and I immediately lose touch with my truth and my Being.

Every act of violence towards others or myself, every expression of anger, bitterness, criticism, jealousy, outrage, resentment, and fear all come from a sense of separateness. Even every time I am annoyed, every time I am judgmental or identify myself with anything less than who I really am, I have contributed to the idea of separateness from God. Whenever I am acting out of competition, boredom, scarcity, or judgment, I add to my sense of separateness. All of these negative energies are reflections of my fear, and when I am living in fear then my ego, my false-self, is in charge of my life.

I do not like to admit it, but my ego eats up a large part of my conscious existence. I am in the consciousness of my ego with every addiction and attachment I am prey to. Every act of gossip, unkindness, jealousy, envy, arrogance, complaint, criticism, sarcasm, every bit of grabbing, protecting, forcefully controlling, and every rationalization or defense of my thoughts and my actions, comes from my ego, my petty little, whiny self.

As soon as I do something contradictory to my Being, I get lost. I become this little contracted ego identity and, most debilitating of all, I think this is who I am. This is what sin is; it is missing the mark. "Missing the mark" is an ancient archery term which the Bible uses to describe sin. What we call sin is not being who I am; it is not acting out of my true Self.

Look at the world today. We are missing the mark all over the place and paying the consequences. Today each one of us has a choice to be the truth of what we are or not. We can contribute to the violence and chaos or to the love and serenity. That choice can be reflected in everything we do and every thought we choose to hold onto.

When I become conscious of a negative thought or action, I need to realize, "Oh, I was unkind; I just added to the fear and hatred in the world." I need to remain conscious so I can either redeem fear and hatred with forgiveness or purposefully act to add to the love and peace of this world.

My true Self is me with no biography or history; it is me with no specific role or function. My true Self is the me beyond all of the usual "I ams," such as "I am male, Leo, minister, teacher, grandfather." The truth of me is clear of all that. My true Self is beyond the drama, the soap operas, beyond my salary, my possessions, and my talents. It is beyond all the ways I normally define myself. When I strip away all the nonessentials I realize my "I am" is God's I Am. It is free from prejudice, fear, hatred, and all the other attachments that keep me stuck in my little ego.

The true Self responds to nothing except God Itself. It responds to and only recognizes love. The ego cannot know God, and the true Self already does.

"I pray that they all may be one. Father! May they be in us, just as you are in me and I am in you. May they be one..." (Jn 17:21)

When I persevere in my commitment to myself to dig deeply through all the stuff, the dramas, the identities, and the roles I play in life, I make the most essential discovery. I discover God. When I search inside of myself and discover God, as my essence and my being, I also discover you there too. I do not occupy the same physical body as you do, but I share the same essence, God's Spirit. In the awareness of the presence of God in all things, I am one with you. There is only one of us here. There is only one of us writing this book. There is only one of us reading. At other times, there is only one of us crying; there is only one of us walking down the street; there is only one of us on the grocery line. I realize you are my brother, my sister. You might be asleep at the moment, but you are trying to wake up as much as I am. The profound truth is if I exclude one person from this awareness, I miss the mark.

Here we are every moment of every day with the choice of living from our God-Self or our ego. It seems like a no-brainer, but it is obviously more difficult than that. How do we live that choice, to be who we really are? We have to be awake to choose God. We have to work on letting go of the importance and even the meaning we put on all the labels in our lives. The reality of our spiritual life has nothing to do with drama, fame, or attention. It does not have anything to do with comparisons or characterizations.

Get to know your true Self. Spend time with yourself. God knows you know your ego well enough; you can talk about it for hours! You choose; you practice; you dedicate yourself to the truth. Dedicate yourself to the law of love; remind yourself, especially in times of turmoil, "There is only one presence and one power in the universe and in my life, God the good omnipotent." Dedicate yourself to staying awake and aware. When you do fall prey to negativity, in whatever form, you affirm to yourself, "This negativity, this limiting thought, is not the truth."

Remind yourself that you are not alone. God's work continues within you to wake you up to the reality of who you are. *A Course in Miracles* asks, "Is it reasonable to think that God presented us with a task and would not provide the means for us to attain it?" In other words, if God has given you this choice to go beyond your limited ego, do you not think He would give you the means to achieve it?

Practice sensing the creative life of God in your bones. Practice gratitude whenever you think of it. Practice whatever else opens your heart whether it is walking in nature, being with children, watching funny movies, cooking, or gardening.

Ask yourself, "What am I passionate about?" Go for it. If you are not passionate about anything, make it your purpose for a while to find it.

Let it set you on fire. If nothing seems to show up for you, be passionate about your search.

Just as an unexpected incident can cause you to contract into that defensive little ego self, know also the thought of your Divine heritage held onto and truly believed can open your heart to encompass all of humanity.

Every act of hatred and fear keeps humanity stuck. Every time I respond to fear and hatred with more fear and hatred I am adding to the stuckness. Whenever there is an act of kindness, of unconditional love, forgiveness, letting go, mercy, compassion, it moves creation forward, and opens the space for more love and kindness.

In our church, we are encouraged to give ourselves the message, "We are divine children of God; God dwells within us." We are urged to remember that there is only One Presence and One Power, God the Good, all Powerful, that our task is to be the purest channel of God's Light, Love, Abundance, and Strength. The challenge is to go beyond the words. Knowing who I am and acting out of that state of consciousness are two very different things.

How do I discover if I am acting from the truth and the heart of who I really am? The clearest answer is that the results of acting from my truth will first change my perspective, and then it will change my world. When my thoughts and actions are focused on positive truths such as love and compassion, I will begin to know them more deeply as true. The more I practice, the more they become a part of me. Just as Jesus did not focus on death, sin, or illness, I will begin to see beyond the hatred and scarcity. I will not judge, but I will see either the love or yearning for love and I will honor that.

I want to know there will be a day when I can open the newspaper or turn on TV and see a world that is loving and free of violence; when the good news attracts more attention than the bad; when the children of the world, our true potential, are getting more attention than celebrities; when the preciousness of the Earth means more to me than a flat-screen TV and a bigger house; when the world's money and resources are going to feeding the hungry and healing the sick instead of making bombs and bullets. Then, then I will know I am living from Truth.

Then I will know I am working from my true Self.

A *Course in Miracles* states: "The Love of God is what created me. The Love of God is everything I am. The Love of God proclaimed me as His Son. The Love of God within me sets me free" (from Lesson 269). "I have no purpose today except to look upon a liberated world, set free of all judgments I have made. Father, this is Your will for me today, and therefore it must be my goal as well" (from Lesson 312).

Do not sell yourself short. You are here to change the world. You are here to redeem the world. It is time you let the God within you, your true Self, out of the closet. It's time for you not to be afraid or hesitant about who you are, and who you are meant to be. When you truly know who you are you will be acting out of that True Self, and the results in yourself and the world will be nothing short of amazing.

Who do you think you are? Remember that one? I would get asked that question as a child when I inadvertently overstepped some unspecified boundary my parents had set. I never had an answer, but I always felt shamed and confused by the question and the tone in which it was delivered. Today, I fantasize on what it would be like if I responded to the question, "Who do you think you are?" by answering with Truth. "I am a child of God, unconditionally loved, full of grace and light. That is who I am. Thank you for asking!"

The spiritual teacher and psychologist Robert Assagioli would begin his guided meditations by saying, "Remember that you have a body, but you are not your body. You have feelings and emotions and you are not your feelings and emotions. You have thoughts and a mind, but you are not your thoughts or your mind. You are much more than that." You are more than your body, emotions, mind, and all the roles you act out. You are much more than all of that.

By the time we reach adolescence we are like an automobile with bumper stickers all over it. We are covered with labels of all the things people have told us we are and all the things we have been told we think we should be. We start believing all these labels. By the time we are verbal, we already have a huge stack of labels stuck to us which we think form our identity.

As we go through life and enter into the stage of spiritual awareness, we begin to discard labels and layers. It is painful; it is surrender. Some roles and identities we can shed without particular difficulty, others are stuck to us like a second skin. Surrender is letting go of who I think I am. Surrender of my little identities allows God and Spirit to define me, instead of letting my ego and the world tell me who I am.

Every moment is a choice, and in order to make that choice I have to do two things; I have to be aware of the choice and I have to surrender, let go, and allow a power greater than my conscious self to lead me to see myself as God sees me.

MEDITATION: ROLES ARE LIKE CLOTHES

As you get comfortable, relaxed, and open,
take a few deep cleansing breaths, opening even more.

Count backwards from ten to one as you breathe deeply.
You can feel a sense of lightness and receptiveness as you allow Spirit to speak to you, sharing with you exactly what you need.

Breathe deeply and experience yourself more and more relaxed as you open to this meditation.

Notice yourself going to a closet. Now you are standing in front of it. This is the closet that contains all your uniforms for all your roles in life. Review for yourself what you are going to do that day.

Each role has a mode of dress or uniform. You can imagine what it is like to put on some of them right now. What do you experience when you identify yourself with a significant role in your life? As you put on the uniform of parent or lawyer or teacher or whatever it might be, notice everything you can. Notice how you hold yourself in your body; notice what you are most aware of. Notice what your major concerns are.

Take the uniform off and now try on another and again notice how you experience yourself in your body, what your concerns are, and anything else you are aware of.

What are the differences you experience between this role and the other?

Now step back from the closet. You have no uniform on at all now.

Who are you? How do you experience yourself when none of these roles are being practiced?

Can you begin to know that even these roles, as important as some of them are, are not *who* you are?

Allow your spiritual knowing to now enter, and begin to know you are an expression of God's unconditional love. That is who you are. That is not a role you play, it is your true identity.

All of your other roles in life are simply various ways you have invented to be an expression of God's unconditional love.

What would it be like to live out of that truth?

Here you are standing in front of your closet. Each uniform represents a different role in your life such as parent or guardian, your work, your play, or your hobbies. You notice that your roles in life range from the very significant to the trivial.

Breathe and know who you are.

Begin to be conscious again of your breathing. Breathe deeply and stretch. Come fully back here in your body, completely centered and grounded.

Get up, stretch, and look around you. Become familiar with the place again, feeling yourself in your body. Journal or process any other way you like.

NUGGETS

I believe one of the unspoken lessons of Jesus is, "You are not who you think you are. You are not your station in life, you are not what society or history has made you, you are not your label or your caste, you are not what you do. You are a child of God."

The separated and isolated self will always feel guilty and insecure.

This stripping away of roles will not happen without silence and solitude.

You can be more in touch with your true Self by asking yourself questions such as, "Where in my life is God obvious to me? Is God most evident to me in music, nature, reading, meditation, dance, or…?"

I can also become attached to my identity as a member of a tribe or family. Again this keeps me safe, but at the price of my own individuality.

Relief from the blame, shame, and guilt of the past is not an invitation to irresponsibility.

Even if my actions were not purposely malicious, my missing the mark has consequences, sometimes substantial ones. I am answerable for the consequences of my actions. If I smashed into your car and said, "Oh, I'm terribly sorry; I didn't mean it," I am sure that would not be enough for you. I would need to give you my insurance card, and eventually be responsible for fixing the damages.

What needs healing? My perception of who I am needs healing.

I am wonderful. I am One with God. I abide in the consciousness of Unity. I do not need healing and neither do you. It is my perception that is warped and wounded.

How quickly I move from the deep spiritual truth that I am a beloved child of God to whatever "realities" my mind and senses are giving me.

My soul tells me I am whole; my senses tell me I am not. Which one am I going to believe?

LETTING GO AND
LETTING LOVE DO ITS WORK

I WAS EXPERIENCING *days upon days of deep darkness. I was surprised I had enough positive energy to put one foot in front of the other, much less go to work, but I did. I woke up one night feeling Margo's hand on my back and hearing her whisper the words, "I love you; I love you." The darkness did not lift, so it seemed as if nothing changed, but everything changed. That is the transformational power of love.*

Have *you* ever been transformed by the power of love? What did you need to let go of? What did you need to let in?

If you have ever wondered about kissing a frog you realize that many of the earliest stories from mythology and folklore were all about the transformational power of love. Unfortunately, we have lost our sense of that wonder. We have reduced the greatest power in the universe to "cute." Instead of being looked upon as the essential element of life, the incredible transformational power of love has become Fantasyland.

If I could paraphrase some thoughts of Jesus, the Master:

"Don't you know; don't you see? The greatest lesson I can give you is not about walking on water, or even forgiveness. Forgiveness is a mere reflection of what I really want to teach you. Above all I come to teach you the transformational power of love."

"What you call miracles of healing the sick and raising the dead are illustrations of that power. Here is how it works in its simplest form. I do not see lepers; I do not see blind people; I do not see sickness or death. I see only life and wholeness and completeness, and by holding this vision of the perfection that you are, that vision becomes manifest. No matter what ideas you or the rest of the world are holding, I am holding you in love, and the love comes through. That is what I mean when I say, 'The gates of hell shall not prevail against it.' (Mt 16:18 NRSV) The gates of hell and all the other negativity you might hold can never prevail against the transformational power of love."

Love transforms; fear stagnates. Why would anyone choose the latter?

In our society's cultivation of the ego we have created a world of fear and cynicism. In the twisted logic of the ego this feels safe. As insane as that sounds, the results of that thinking are all around us: nuclear proliferation, corporate greed, billions spent on military force.

Fearful thoughts as well as those of lack and scarcity also affect us as individuals. All we have to do is observe the outrageous divorce rate, rampant consumerism, and drug use and alcoholism. Any time we think we are not enough or we do not have enough, we will work and obsess to get more. We will hold on tighter, and become more and more wrapped up in our self-centered, terrified little ego.

When we are identified with our frightened little ego, we tend to recreate negative and fearful experiences. We have no problem at all dredging up old experiences of guilt, shame, or fear. When it comes to positive experiences, however, we seem to be resistant. We will say to ourselves or others, "Yeah, that was great, but it was a long time ago," or, "As much as I enjoyed that (trip, carnival, or dinner) to keep going back there is just living in the past."

A few years ago, I was studying hypnosis with a master teacher,

Ron Klein. He taught us a wonderful exercise called "Creating a Resource State of Mind." In it, we were encouraged to relax, and then bring to mind a time in our life when we were doing "something we loved doing and doing it very well." The circumstances did not have to be elaborate or dramatic. It could be something as simple as cooking a meal, reading a special book, or listening to a favorite piece of music. Then we practiced connecting to this state of mind and even turning up the energy on the experience. We would be reminded this is not simply a memory; we are actually creating a space to live from the energy of that experience.

Part of the learning was that no matter what circumstances might be occurring, the energy of that positive experience was still present and could be brought up and used anytime. That was simply amazing to me. Then I realized I do this all the time with negative experiences and feelings. I can become guilty and fearful in a heartbeat. I can think of something troublesome in my past, even though it does not touch my life now, and BAM! I am right back in it, and it might have happened fifteen years ago.

I find my tendency to lock onto negative energy especially troublesome when I am experiencing peace and happiness and my ego-mind turns in on itself and says, "Should you really be feeling this good? There must be something you need to worry about, be afraid of, or feel guilty about." Sure enough, I will find something. If there is nothing in the present, then I can dig up something from the past, and inevitably I will move from peace and happiness to depressed and awful.

We are continually creating either positive or negative resource states of mind in our consciousness based on the thoughts we are holding onto. One of the amazing things about this process of creating a resource is that it has very little to do with what is happening outside of us.

There is an old metaphysical adage that "energy follows thought," and this whole sense of creating resources is part of that truth. The transformational power of love flows from the loving, joyful, peaceful thoughts we choose to hold. I choose which thoughts I will hold onto. I am becoming more and more aware of how important that choice is, to me personally and to the world.

If the positive transforming power of love were a brush, then my wife Margo would be an artist. If she is experiencing herself as down, fearful, or stuck in any form of negativity, she brings to mind thoughts of peace, gratitude, and joy. She thinks about our grandkids, walking in nature, or someone's smile. She is not denying the negative nor is she living in the past; she is deciding what energies she is going to focus on. She is tapping into the positive energies that already exist inside of her. She is not giving in to the distractions and destructive thinking that negativity can produce.

When I am in a down place I have the tendency to trash myself even more. Margo once asked me, "Why would I ever want to make myself feel worse? Why would I kick myself when I am down?" I did not have an answer to that one. I know I was not attempting to make myself feel worse, even though that was the result. What I was doing was allowing my feelings of worthlessness to control my thoughts and actions. I am still learning to use the power of love the way she does.

One of the many beautiful aspects about life-changing and transformational experiences is that their energy is always with you. Even if the event of transformation is long past, the positive energy of that experience is still with you. It is a part of you, not just as a memory, but a real part of you. When you choose to focus on an experience of the transformational power of love in your life, you are not living in the past; you are actually bringing the experience into the present. You are creating a present moment pregnant with joy and positive energy.

A peak experience for me a few years ago was attending a concert by my favorite musical group, the Moody Blues. The joy and excitement of that concert still lives in my body. All I have to do is put on a recording of *The Question,* and I realize the vibrant energy is still there inside me. I am not living in the past; I am not simply resurrecting an old memory. I am allowing myself to be consciously aware of an energy and experience that remain very much alive within me. I can energize myself with inner experiences by bringing to mind a hug, the laughter of a grandchild, a piece of music, a photograph, or anything that turns me on.

Life will really come at me at times, and there will be hairy and difficult situations to work with. During these times I want to have my positive resources available to me. I need to be open to those positive energies which live inside me. I need to practice experiencing the power of that positive energy. I do not want to wait until a crisis happens. I might be too off balance then. If I want to live out of the power of love then I have to practice connecting with and expressing that transformational power within me. Through awareness, I can catch the negativity before I become mired in it. I can become aware of judgment, criticism, blame, guilt, and all of those other energy-draining thoughts and work on turning them around. I remember that I can choose the thoughts I hold onto. Just like that wonderful commercial, "I could have had a V-8," I can remind myself, "I could see peace instead of conflict; I could see love instead of hatred; I could see joy instead of bitterness." Again, these are not just words; these statements are affirmations of the transformational power of love that exists inside of me.

Life can come at any of us with an illness or other legitimate concerns. There could be a sickness or tragedy in the life of a loved one such as a lost job, a child or grandchild who is ill, or a loved one in a difficult circumstance. When life hits us, rather than becoming mired in negativity and despair, by working with our positive resources as often as possible, we will be much more in the flow of the God-given power within us. We have all kinds of resources inside us, both positive and negative. We can choose the kind of energy we focus on and create for ourselves.

How do I hold tragedy and difficult circumstances? Do I view the hard events of life as punishment or learning? Do I respond to these situations as a victim or as an active participant in the solution?

Remember my friend Molly asking the question, "What's the lesson here?" I can also ask, "What can I learn from this? What is being challenged in me? What is my growing edge? What is the love in me being called to do?"

We might also find ourselves challenged to ask, "Where is the love here?" We might have practiced being conscious of the power of love, but in some life circumstances it might be difficult to find any love at all. What I need to realize is that I might not be able to find the love in the situation, but I can know the love is inside of you and me. The significant question is not, "Where is the love in this situation?" but "Where is the love in me?" or, "Where is God in me?" As I practice finding God and finding love, I will be able to see God in practically everything. I will recognize the moments when I am not seeing God, and pull myself out of that negative projection into a more positive one.

There have been times in my life when my experiences of hurt and negativity have felt much more powerful than the energies of unity consciousness and healing. As I sat and wrestled with those experiences, I began to realize if the negativity were more powerful than the transformational power of love, then I would have been done in a long time ago. I came to the startling conclusion that whatever my senses, memory, or emotions were telling me was just not true on the spiritual plane. If the powers of darkness were greater, which was what my emotions and experience were telling me, then they would have overcome me a long time ago.

Isn't that amazing? *The darkest, most difficult times in our lives, when we thought and felt that we could not move on, the times when we felt the darkness was overpowering, even in those moments, the Light, the Power of Spirit was stronger.* Remember that.

Positive energy produces more positive energy. I have spent too much time focusing on what is *not* working in my life, and attempting to change it. What happens when I dwell on what I do not have or what is not working? I lose energy; I become more negative; I become discouraged at my lack of success; I think there must be something wrong with me; I become guilty and depressed. I still do not rid myself of what is not working, and I have created a whole new truckload of negative baggage besides. I have given the negativity more energy.

I am becoming more enamored with a rather simple practice, "Work with what is working." Work with what is already working, as minuscule as it might be. Nurture it; feed it; help it to grow. "I'm never happy," you might say. "I always look at the down side of things." If those statements were totally true, you would have checked out a long time ago. You might not have moments of stupendous happiness, but if you examine your life there will be a few things that amuse you or almost bring a smile to your face. Concentrate on those things; find more of them.

The negative thoughts projected by your ego-consciousness are usually all-or-nothing thoughts such as, "I never..." or "It always happens this way." There are very few absolutes in life. The stuff of living is always on a continuum and is measured as a matter of degree rather than all or nothing.

"I don't love myself," you might hear yourself saying to a therapist. "Well," your therapist might say, "you love yourself enough to come here to deal with your life. You love yourself enough to get out of bed this morning, to bathe, to groom yourself, to have breakfast, and to put your seat belt on." Begin to become aware of the areas and actions in your life that reflect even the slightest bit of self-love; become more and more conscious of them and dedicate yourself to working with what is already working.

These aspects of your life that are already working for you might seem to be insignificant, but they are not meaningless. It is upon the little things that are already working in your life that you can build.

One of the simplest yet most profound questions I have been asking myself lately, before speaking or acting, is, "Will this word or action open my heart or close it?" When I am conscious enough, I can physically feel a negative thought or word shut down my heart. "Does it open my heart or close it?" Asking the question, opening to grace, drawing on the positive resources within, and taking action are powerful ways of reinforcing the transformational power of love.

Can I focus on the transformational power of love that is within me? Can I go beyond how insignificant my ego thinks I am to the greatness and the power that my true essence, the God within me, expresses?

We know love transforms. When we are gentle and loving towards ourselves, no matter what else is happening, our lives are easier and smoother. I can be in a down mood and think of my grandson's smiling face, and for a moment at least I am free. Each one of us has been and is continually being transformed by the power of love. Imagine how many people are praying for you at this moment, many whom you do not even know. Just the power of that thought is transforming.

The power of love transforms us by bringing us closer to the truth of who we are. The power of love transforms us by bringing us closer to the truth of who we are. If God is Love and God and the Kingdom of God dwells within us, then we are love as well. That is it. That is who we are. That is why love remains. That is why "the greatest of these is love." (1 Co 13:13) When faith and hope are no longer necessary, love remains, not the yearning for love, not the love that is desirous of completion, but the love that offers peace. In love, the Love of God from whom all love emanates, there is no yearning, and no movement because there is nothing to get or to move towards. We are home.

MEDITATION: LETTING LOVE TRANSFORM

(This is another practice which can be done easily at different times during the day without formality.)

As you get comfortable, relaxed, and open, take a few deep cleansing breaths, opening even more.

Count backwards from ten to one as you breathe deeply. You can feel a sense of lightness and receptiveness as you allow Spirit to speak to you, sharing with you exactly what you need.

Breathe deeply and experience yourself more and more relaxed as you open to this meditation.

"Be ye transformed by the renewal of your mind," said Paul. (Ro 12:2 NRSV)

Work on looking at something or someone differently.

Notice something in your life you have attempted to change by brute force, pushing, pushing, and pushing.

Notice how exhausting and frustrating that is. Notice how you were either trying to do it all by yourself or attempting to make your prayer come out the way you thought it should.

Hold a gentle image of what you desire to transform within yourself.

As you prayerfully let go, ask for your highest good and the grace to open yourself to that blessing. Gently let go of preconceived outcomes. Know that God is aware of both your need and your desire. Let go, trust.

Begin to be conscious again of your breathing. Breathe deeply and stretch. Come fully back here in your body, completely centered and grounded.

Get up, stretch, and look around you. Become familiar with the place again, feeling yourself in your body. Journal or process any other way you like.

NUGGETS

We haven't really been changing the world yet; we think we are too small and too insignificant.

What would it be like if I looked at this lovingly?

If you could see with the eyes of God what would you see?

The power of love is generated through the power of choice.

Love is expressed in how we respond.

You cannot act from beyond your present level of consciousness.

Ask yourself, "Am I in survival mode? Am I thinking or acting out of fear, anger, hurt, defensiveness, or scarcity?"

Am I so identified with my feelings and my thoughts and the role I am in right now that I cannot see anything else? (Are you just someone reading a book?)

Negativity in the form of anger, hatred, fear, or any other mode does not transform; it destroys.

As Martin Luther King, Gandhi, and others have said, "Darkness cannot drive away darkness."

We are constantly creating either positive or negative states of mind with our thoughts.

It is work to keep the power of love in conscious focus, and the work pays off.

To remember or reminisce is a gentle luxury that can be quite pleasing. Remembrances shared are healthy when we do not live in the past. Connecting or engaging with an experiential state of mind is not a reminiscence; it is acknowledging and using an energy within.

This thing we call Grace is the choice to put our love into action. Love asks, "How can I do this differently?"

Because I have the tendency to gravitate towards negative thoughts, I need to be doubly vigilant.

How do I approach life? Is someone always doing something to me, or do I approach life's difficulties with the attitude that it is my job to do something with it?

LOVING ME, LOVING YOU

FOR SUCH A *long time, I thought other people were supposed to fix me and complete me. That was what relationships were all about. Find the right friends and partner and I will be happy. Of course other people thought I could fix them and make them complete as well. That never worked either.*

We are all related; we are all dependent on one another, but close relationships offer a unique and sometimes difficult challenge to growth. The first challenge is to get beyond the ego, and if you are like me, this challenge will last a lifetime.

What happens when we meet simply as egos in a relationship? When egos meet they rub against one another; that is what egos do. That friction produces a whole spectrum of feelings and reactions: annoyance, anger, fear, judgment, just to name a few. When a person is made out to be an object or a thing, the ego is in charge of the perception. Using only the perception of the ego, the other person is either an opponent, someone to be controlled, or is looked upon as irrelevant.

Because intimacy stretches me, the process is not always comfortable. One of the first things that comes about when I commit to an intimate relationship is that all of my unfinished business comes right up in my face. The unfinished matters of my life include feelings I have never dealt with, shame I have never looked at, woundedness I have never healed, grieving I have not finished, along with addictions and other compulsive behaviors. They all come up, like magma bubbling up from the earth's core. Often, I am so focused on how great I feel being in love, I am taken by surprise when all these issues blast to the surface of my consciousness.

There have been numerous times when I have worked with couples who have been ambushed by this phenomenon, and often the realization seems to hit right after the literal honeymoon. This is because the ritual of marriage is a way of voicing to the world that the couple are in a committed relationship and commitment is a dirty word to the ego. When the ego feels itself trapped all hell breaks loose.

The suddenness and force with which my previously submerged issues hit me generates fear and a tremendous amount of defensiveness, along with one of the ego's major forms of defense: called projection. The ego's projection could sound like: "Well, I never felt this way until I met you." "This was never a problem until I married you." "It's not me, it's you." "Well, you started it." "Well, if you hadn't brought it up, then I wouldn't have had to say that."

The ego in its fear and limited perspective creates other and more subtle ways of hindering relationships. We need to be aware that this fearful little piece of ourselves is only trying to protect itself. Although practically everything is a threat to the ego, the commitment to love is one of the greatest.

Many relationships fail because we experience ourselves as unlovable. We cannot believe that someone can love us the way we are, and so we both consciously and unconsciously sabotage the relationship. We wind up playing some unconscious games such as "Come Closer; Go Away." It unfolds like this: I let you come close to me because I am comfortable being open and vulnerable at this moment, but as soon as you get close I get frightened and I do something to push you away. Then I feel the deep need to be loved and accepted by you so I let myself be open and vulnerable once more, and the cycle continues.

I discovered myself playing this game in my early relationship with Margo. I recall soon after we had met, I told her, "I could come and visit you sometime," and feeling very open and free saying that. Then she responded, "Yes, and I could come and visit you, too." Well, that just freaked me out. Looking back, everything was wonderful when I felt as if I were in control of things, but when I felt another person making decisions that affected me, I became contracted and fearful. I wanted to be close to Margo but on my terms, so I let her into my heart for a while, got frightened and shut down again. The "game" continued until I became aware of my fear. I had to make some conscious choices. Since my emotions are fairly fickle, I knew I could not feel safe all the time, but I knew in my heart I am safe with Margo. I began to make more choices with my heart rather than my fear.

As I became more conscious of my fears I also realized I was not consciously or maliciously pushing her away. I was frightened and acting out of that scared, contracted self, the ego. When I realized I was "in prison" I began to make some choices to get out.

Another fearful ego game is called, "Will You Love Me If..." It unfolds something like this: "I'm not sure that anyone could really love me, so I have to keep testing things out. I do something outrageous to see if you can still love me when I am stupid, forgetful, or obnoxious. I am very pleased when I discover that you still love me after that, but then I have to push the envelope a little more and a little more." When the other person finally gives up I can say, "See, I knew you didn't love me."

The ego thinks in terms of scarcity, that there will not be enough. It thinks there will not be enough love, or enough happiness, or enough attention to go around. With scarcity thinking in tow, the frightened ego intrudes again and begins to spawn competition between partners. Sometimes, unknowingly, we begin to "count up points." Conscious or unconscious thoughts such as, "Well, I'll let you have your way this time, but next time you better let me have mine." The issue could be sex, money, or even taking out the garbage. The destructive results of point counting and competition quickly make us enemies rather than lovers and friends.

A popular phrase in the sixties was, "If you can't love yourself, you can never love anyone else." That message really got me. I did not feel very lovable. I did not think I loved myself very much, but I also knew I cared for some other people very deeply. How could I love someone else when I did not love myself? I could not get it.

I finally realized this idea of loving myself and others was not an absolute. When I put the focus back on myself, I realize that my ability to truly love more unconditionally is measured by my ability to love myself, but this is not an all-or-nothing proposition. Loving myself, as with many other internal abilities, is a matter of degree. My ability to love myself is like a magnifying glass that channels my ability to love you. We all have the ability to love ourselves to some degree; the more powerful the lens the more powerful the love that comes through.

As I continue to work on making the conscious choice to go beyond the limits of my ego, I also realize the need to have a good relationship with myself is linked to having a good relationship with you. If my relationship with myself stinks, my relationship with you is not going to smell very good either. Once I begin to work on conscious self-love and respect, I become more aware of who I am and also what I can give. Relationships teach me what I need to give of myself and by doing so teach me what I can give to others.

The ego teaches you that the world is not a safe place, and love especially is not safe. It is challenging to live beyond the ego and to live outside that safety and self-imposed scarcity. The ego thinks to love unconditionally is to make yourself into a doormat. The soul knows that to love unconditionally is the only way to love. If you have ever experienced loving someone completely, you know that unconditional love does not destroy you; on the contrary, it makes you stronger. When you encounter the ego's fear of loving, do not argue with it; let go of the fear. The ego does not remember that unconditional love is good, but the heart does. Listen to your heart, not your fear.

Intimacy pushes us to grow in love with those close to us, but intimacy also presents us with a model of how to relate to everyone. The way Jesus stated it, "For if you love those who love you what reward do you have? Do not even tax collectors do the same?" (Mt 5:46 ESV)

It is natural to think some relationships are more special than others, but one of the many lessons relationships can teach us is how to love *everyone* deeply and honestly. Spiritually speaking, there are no special relationships, or better said, *all* relationships are special. As I continue to stretch and grow, I am asked to love everyone with equal devotion.

When I first encountered the concept that "there are no special relationships" in *A Course in Miracles*, I thought the idea was ridiculous. "Of course," I said to myself, "my relationship with Margo and her children and our grandchildren is special." Then I realized, in a moment of insight, I was being asked to love everyone as deeply as I love my wife and grandchildren.

"Who is my neighbor?" Jesus was asked. His reply via the parable of the Good Samaritan was, "Everyone." Spiritually, my love for Margo, Mikayla, Paige, Meaghan, Aoife, or Fionn gives me a reference point of how I am being asked to love everyone. Love everyone, be they government officials, terrorists, rude clerks, or people who are talking behind me at the movie. Love everyone the way you love those you know you love. The other person is ultimately God, no matter what form he or she might be wearing today.

The challenge becomes "Who don't you see as God and why not?" To answer that question we must enter into the consciousness of the soul. We have already looked at some of the things that occur when we meet one another on an ego level. What happens when people meet one another on a soul level?

When we meet as souls on a journey, when we recognize one another as spiritual beings, we are one and we know it; we are loved and we know it. We are the living embodiment of the Golden Rule.

Buddha said it this way, "See yourself in others. Who then shall you harm?"

There are many interpretations of what occurs when we fall in love. Some would suggest that we are simply in love with an image of ourselves, like Narcissus staring at his reflection in the water. Scott Peck suggests falling in love is a "mild form of insanity." Both of those are true at times. I would also like to think that when we fall in love we are meeting one another on the level of the soul. We do not simply experience a lack of ego boundaries; I believe we are relating to one another as soul to soul. The difficulty lies in the fact that we do not stay there.

Because, in our human existence, we continually cope with issues of both ego and soul, it is not surprising that most of our relationships have aspects of both.

When I am with clients, I am pointedly focused on them. I am listening intently, making eye contact, and being aware of body language. I am also letting go of judgment and lovingly honoring their process as I create a space for them to heal. What is amazing to me is that as soon as I walk in the door of my home, my focus immediately shifts to my wants and my needs and creating a safe place for me to be in. Even though my intention is to be kind, unselfish, and loving, when I lose focus and let my self-centered needs take over, my original goals seem to vanish. When I lose my intention, focus, and sense of commitment, my wife could be talking to me, but I am thinking about dinner, or reading the paper, or programming my DVR. When I lose my focus and intention, my fearful, protective, self-centered ego takes over automatically.

I can choose to practice focus and intention. When I am home, I want to be aware I am with someone I love, not someone I am in competition with, not someone who wants to get over on me, not someone who is trying to hurt me, or take something away from me. How often do I lose that awareness when I am wrapped up in myself and my own needs?

I often wonder, "If loving is so good, and wonderful, and beautiful, and healing, why do we keep going back to the ego-consciousness of fear, competition, and scarcity thinking?" The answer is simply that the ego always wants to get back in control. Even when we have surrendered our self-centered fear and choose to focus on loving, the ego remains fearful. The ego's desire to be safe and fulfilled is still present.

Not only does the ego project all its hidden issues on the other person, it also projects its wants and needs onto the other person as well. This is another reason why we fall back into ego-consciousness so easily, because we always have wants and needs that we want to be satisfied, and it is much easier to have someone else do the work for us. It is such an easy thing to expect another to heal us or to make us feel better or complete us.

We all have unhealed places, and healing is a major factor in relationships. But if I just come to you in my woundedness with the desire that you fix me, the relationship will not work. If I just come to you in strength in order to fix you, it will not work. I have to come to you acknowledging my woundedness, and loving you in yours. I also have to come to you in strength to be willing to help you heal, and be open to letting your strength help heal me. A partnership embraces one another's wholeness, and also acknowledges my own.

Even though relationships involve other people, they truly are about discovering who we are, and the ultimate goal of all relationships is that we see God in the beloved and let them see God in us. When someone loves us, they help to create a space, a safe haven, where we can heal and grow. This space is unconditional; it is free of guilt and shame and expectations. We give this space to one another. Imagine what that would be like. Two people creating a loving safe space where they can heal. That is what love is, that is the essence of relationship.

Ultimately, on the spiritual path of relationships, we are encouraged to cultivate our intuitive heart. It is not with the mind or the senses that we know what is healthy and what is not. It is with the heart.

Not all relationships are going to work. Even Jesus had problems with some people. The ultimate authority for going or staying is your heart, not your codependent unhealthy needs, but your heart.

There have been so many people I have worked with who have told me that at some point in a relationship there was a voice or sensation inside that said, "Uh-oh, this is not good," but then they purposely overlooked that inner advice or told themselves they could handle it.

Here is a very simple rule: If you are honestly working on your own health and well-being, and a relationship is constantly draining you of energy, then it is probably unhealthy and you are probably trying to satisfy unhealthy needs in yourself or the other. The only solution is to let go. If you want to get rid of those lumps on your head stop running into the wall.

The heart is fearless, but it is not stupid. It knows when it is time to stay or time to go. Unlike the ego, the heart does not judge or blame. It accepts responsibility for its own stuff and the problems it has created.

Good working relationships, be they friendships or more intimate ones, are always equal to equal, eyeball to eyeball. We might bring different gifts, but we never need to expect our partner to give in to us. It is never about winners or losers. It is never about you or me; it is about us. There is a great scene in the movie *Rocky* that really touched me. It is the night before his big fight, and he goes to the auditorium, looks over the ring, and has a talk with the promoter. He goes back home to his crappy old apartment, and sits on the side of the bed where his girlfriend Adrian is sleeping. He mutters out loud, waking her, "I can't do it, I can't beat him." Adrian sits up, looks at Rocky, and asks, "What are we going to do?" Not "Oh, that's terrible, what are you going to do?" but, "What are *we* going to do?" That's beautiful!

MEDITATION: LOVING RELATIONSHIPS

As you get comfortable, relaxed, and open,
take a few deep cleansing breaths,
opening even more.

Count backwards from ten to one as you breathe deeply.
You can feel a sense of lightness and receptiveness as you allow Spirit
to speak to you, sharing with you exactly what you need.

Breathe deeply and experience yourself more and more relaxed as you
open to this meditation.

Relationships provide a safe space for us to heal and grow.

Imagine what it would be like to be in a space that you experience as
being as perfectly safe as you can. You can create any image or set of
sensations you like. You could tune into a natural environment or one
you create yourself.

Right now all the tools for this creation are within your grasp. Take some
time to create this sacred, safe place for yourself.

Pause...

Now within the energy of this safe place, know that the Power and Spirit
of God dwell here with you. You are more than safe; you are enfolded in
the grace and strength and healing power of the infinite.

Pause...

Something needs to heal within you now. Let it come to your consciousness. You do not need to try and think about it, just let it come to you. It
might be something you have been aware of for some time, or what surfaces might be a bit of surprise. You can come back to this place as often
as you choose to heal. For now, simply accept what comes up for you.

Notice your feelings without becoming overly involved in them, and then if you choose to, offer this thing in your life that needs healing, offer it to God.

Let it go, release it. Know you are being healed at this moment. Let it go, and as you let it go breathe into the more open space that now exists within you. Allow it to fill with light and love and grace. Yes. Releasing, healing, and filling up.

Begin to be conscious again of your breathing. Breathe deeply and stretch. Come fully back here in your body, completely centered and grounded.

Get up, stretch, and look around you. Become familiar with the place again, feeling yourself in your body. Journal or process any other way you like.

NUGGETS

Many of us have formed relationships that are based on fixing the other person, or we have worked very hard to attract a person we think will heal us or make us whole. That doesn't work!

A loving relationship is based on creating space and holding a space where the other can do the healing work on themselves. I hold a space; I do not fix; I let go of my defenses.

Just being there for someone makes a difference.

Even though the limited consciousness of the ego can hinder intimacy, we do not intend to kill the ego off. The ego is not the enemy here.

When I think the ego's limited perception is the truth, that is when the problems begin.

In response to a barrage of ego-centered fear, the practice of awareness and self-honesty will help me to grow with the challenge of facing my unfinished business. I need to accept that this is *my* stuff and not the other person's. Not only is it mine, but it is mine to work on.

When you recognize the effort being made by another person to stretch and grow, acknowledge that effort and compliment them on it. You will be amazed at the positive energy that flows from that tiny effort.

Human relationships are beautiful as they are, but the spiritual dimension gives them even more meaning and purpose.

Don't hesitate to ask yourself the question, "What is my heart telling me?"

Recognize that building a relationship is a life-long task. I do not want to wait until I have all my stuff together before I get into a relationship. If that were true there would not be any relationships.

Meet one another as souls on a journey rather than egos who are in competition.

Intimate relationships are the crucible for transformation.

Love yourself no matter what.

Let go of your little self in order to truly embrace the other person and your own soul.

See God in yourself and the other until you see only God.

To love well, you must give up your self-centeredness.

Become a sensitive listener, hearing what is said and not said.

Healthy relationships need always to be based on freedom and choice.

Make it a choice, as often as you like, to postpone personal gratification to meet the needs of another. When it is your choice, you can be a lover rather than a codependent victim.

We cannot always choose who we meet or the people or situations we encounter, but we can choose how we respond to them.

You can choose to be as close or intimate with another human being as you want to be, and to that degree you will be challenged to grow. Everything intensifies, the closer, the more intimate, and the more vulnerable we choose to be.

We are here together to honor one another's wholeness, and by doing so we empower one another to heal. Our focus can be on wholeness rather than woundedness.

Know that whatever yearnings are touched off in you by a relationship are fundamentally yearnings for wholeness, Oneness, and union with Spirit.

All relationships have as their purpose to become aware of our Oneness.

A relationship is there to serve one another's opening to love.

Healthy relationships are there to provide a safe place to heal, grow, and transform.

Relationships make us look at our fears, not just the fears of the ego but the fears that have been implanted in us, our woundedness.

LOVING WITHOUT LIMITS

I WANT TO LOVE *you, not be attached to you. I want to create a space for you to grow and heal, and I want you to create that space for me. As much as I might want to heal you, I need to know I cannot do your healing or growth for you.*

When you are in pain I want to understand; I want to offer you comfort and support, even though I cannot take your pain away. I also want to understand and empathize at those times when you want me to fix you even though you know I cannot.

I want to love you without controlling you. I want to honor your journey and love you where you are while continuing to open a space for your becoming.

I want to flow. I want to flow with life.

All attachments are fantasies, not realities. My experiences as I was being influenced by an attachment were real, but the fantasy at the root of any attachment is the illusion of control. I become trapped by my attempts to control something I cannot.

When I step into the attachment trap my world gets thrown off balance. I find myself focusing on the object of my attachment rather than God, the Source, and then I lose track of myself. I lose touch with my soul because I am so identified with the object of my attachment.

Whether it is a person–such as a child, spouse, parent, boss, friend–a place such as home or office, or a thing such as alcohol, drugs, money, sex, or gambling, attachment is an attempt at ownership or control, but what is really holding the reins here? The trap comes as soon as I say, "It is mine and I am not letting go of it." I am really saying, "It is still controlling me; I am not controlling it." I do not like to hear that, but it is true. The catch is I am not willing to admit or accept my powerlessness. My attempts at control create some of the reasons I stay attached so long.

Controlling is manipulating. We are all familiar with methods used to attempt to control others; we all know what buttons to push, what strings to pull, or what we need to do or say to get someone to do what we want. If we want to stop controlling, then we need to stop manipulating. We need to let go and let be.

Controlling is a way of trying to be better than the other person. I am no better or worse than you. I would have no reason to be attached to you or try to control you unless I was holding onto the belief that you are a threat or that I am better than you. If I want to stop controlling, I look at you as being an equal.

Another way of controlling is blaming. "It's all your fault." "If you would only…." What a powerful attachment blame can be. It removes all responsibility from me.

Control is a reflection of wanting to be right, whatever difference that makes. I know I have enjoyed the dubious pleasure of being right. I presume the reason why it feels so pleasurable comes from my ego; it makes me feel as if I am one up on you. Similar to other self-centered pleasures, I get a few moments of self-centered satisfaction, and then emptiness or shame coupled with the need to fill up my insatiable ego again. Although it is not my conscious intention, I have also alienated you as well.

Controlling makes us into victims. We give our power away. It is subtle; it is insane, but true nonetheless. Our attachments own us. We think we are the person in power, but we are really giving our power away to this person, place, or thing we have become attached to.

When I realize I am in prison, I can begin to get out. When I realize I have lost touch with my Source and my own soul, I can begin to get them back.

Detachment is another word for surrender. I make a choice to detach when I realize my attachment is not doing for me what I want it to do; when I realize it never did; when I realize it is now getting in the way, and preventing me from doing or dealing with life situations in a positive, constructive way.

Surrender begins when I become sick and tired of being sick and tired; when I become so totally aware of my entrapment that I can no longer deny it. As the process unfolds I begin to embrace this addiction/attachment, as distasteful as it might be. I embrace this thing as part of me. My awareness leads me to acceptance which leads me to surrender, to letting go, and detachment. Detachment and surrender are processes; they occur deep in my being. I can do all the conscious work necessary to lead me to this place of letting go, but the surrender itself is a deep process of the soul that takes place beyond the level of conscious thought and conscious awareness.

I do not like to think of myself as a controlling person, but I am. Along with exercise, shower, and meditation I attempt to begin every day with a sense of openness. As long as everything goes along with my plan (even though I did not realize I had a plan), I am calm, serene, and very easy to get along with. If a gremlin should enter in the form of a missed appointment, a computer crash, or something as trivial as an unexpected phone call, I can find myself anxious, annoyed, upset, and very off balance. What happened? Something occurred outside of my realm of control, my unconscious plan for the day has been disrupted, and I am paying the price for my need to control when all these negative feelings and thoughts start raging through me.

I have a choice to keep trying to control or to let go; to keep banging my head against the wall or find a door to open. There is substantial power around this sense of choice. Choice creates freedom. Freedom promotes growth. Growth encourages even more detachment. Being stuck allows for very few choices and results in addiction, stagnation, and limitation.

If you want to stop controlling, look at where control plays a role in the many aspects of your life, and break those chunks down into smaller bits and work on them. Instead of attempting to eliminate all your concerns about control at once, focus on one of these issues such as judging, victimhood, blame, manipulation. A good starting point is to look at the situations in your life that knock you off center or drain you of power. These control issues could be related to people, places, things, old ideas, or character defects. When you give your power away you become a victim. Reclaiming your spiritual power can give you the strength and wisdom you need to initiate deep healing and transformation.

If you want to stop controlling, do not beat yourself up because you discover you *are* controlling. Gently let go of the controlling thoughts and behaviors. For instance, if it is judgment that gets in your way, then focus on loving. Love makes room for healing. In Christian scripture, as well as other spiritual traditions, we are told of the dangers of judging. "Judge not, and you shall not be judged"; and in the Lord's Prayer we pray "forgive us our trespasses as we forgive those who trespass against us." Many of us might not realize we say those words every day, and we wonder why we feel guilty or why we do not feel forgiven.

The inner process that leads to detachment is one of self-honest awareness. Before conscious awareness comes to us, there is usually some sense of pain and discomfort that begins to push us to change. Now we bring that awareness to a conscious level. Looking, observing, evaluating, without being pulled apart by judgments, that is detached awareness.

I can be "asleep" even when I am awake. From the second I become conscious in the morning, a cacophony of voices is greeting me. Each thought is telling me how necessary it is, and each thought is accompanied by an emotion. There are countless thoughts attempting to get my attention. They are all yelling at me, saying, "Listen to me; I'm important!"

"Oh, I really don't feel like getting up. I worked hard yesterday. I deserve a little extra rest. Nobody appreciates me. I need to get the air conditioning fixed. I have to go to the bathroom. How much time do I need if I punch the snooze alarm again?" No hot water. Good coffee. Traffic jam. Boss is angry. Stock options are up. Missed lunch. Co-worker brought me a donut. On and on my day unfolds and I am ping-ponged by feelings and events that I have little or no control over.

Detachment means stepping back from the self and looking at your life as a movie. You are the director; you choose what your experiences mean. Step out of your own little melodrama and look at yourself doing whatever it is you are doing. Sometimes you can be so wrapped up in your own little reality that you cannot see anything else. You can be so self-absorbed that you are constantly being manipulated by everything around you and not even realizing it.

Detachment with love is sometimes all I can do. Sheldon Kopp, a gifted author and teacher, gave a wonderful definition of love: "Love is sometimes living with the helpless knowing that we can do nothing about another person's pain." I can be there for that person, but I cannot take away their pain. The knowing that I cannot take away another's pain can pull me in many directions. I think it is one of the reasons why visiting ill people and grieving families is so difficult for some of us. I carry with me the realization that I can do nothing for their pain here on this material plane, and this realization can bring a sense of helplessness that none of us likes to feel. When I love someone I want to be able to take the pain away, to kiss it and make it better, and sometimes I cannot.

No one likes being in pain; no one enjoys knowing someone we love is in pain. It is only natural to want to "fix it." I do not ignore the pain of another when I detach, but I do realize my limits as to what I can do. If someone comes into my office and they are in pain because a lot of emotional stuff is coming to the surface, I am not going to say, "Good! I'm glad you're in pain; it is just what you need and maybe you will learn from that." I know I cannot fix it, but I might be able to give them some ways of working through it; I might be able to offer some help in getting the feelings out and relieving the pain without denying it.

Sometimes we confuse loving with enabling. When I do not allow a person to experience the consequences of their actions, I enable them to continue with the same negative behavior. As a loving human being I am normally going to choose to alleviate or lessen someone's pain if I can; as a loving, growing human being I need to make a distinction between rescuing and truly being helpful. When I attempt to rescue another I become enmeshed in the other person's denial and cover-up. As Kopp states in his definition, sometimes the most loving thing I can do is simply be there.

As I look back on my own life, many incidents of healing that stand out for me are not times when people *did* things for me or told me what to do, but simply when they were there for me. The psychologist Carl Rogers says that "the moment of therapeutic healing" takes place when the counselor/therapist is completely focused on the other person; when the therapist becomes "egoless." When the therapist is not thinking about what the problem is or what to say next, but is simply totally and fully present to the other person, that is when healing takes place. Obviously, being fully focused and present is not limited to therapeutic situations. A primary aspect of spiritual life is the cultivation of the practice of egoless presence with everyone.

Detachment does not mean being callous or hard or being a rock. It does not mean shutting off the tender loving part of ourselves; it means that we do not have to take on the burden of another; we can empathize but we do not have to attempt to take on another's pain.

Here is a core truth: there is no such thing as detaching with love. Detaching *is* loving; they are the same thing. Detaching is love of myself as well as love of the other; I love you and I am going to give you the space to grow. I love you and I am going to give up my attempts to control you. Detachment with love is another way of describing unconditional love. Unconditional love is really the only kind of love there is. Unconditional love without limits is the love that loves no matter what. It is the love that states emphatically, "I love you just the way you are." Most of us are not taught how to receive this kind of love, and so we do not know how to give it either. Most of us were taught the ways of conditional love, which is not really love at all. The voice of conditional love will state, "I will love you if...," and "I will love you because..." Unconditional love is freeing and understanding; it is neither grasping nor controlling.

Take a moment and examine some other words and concepts that express detachment to get more of a feel for what detachment is. Some other terms are letting go; surrender; tough love; and turning it over. Just get a feel for those words and the sensations they might evoke.

AN EXPERIENCE OF LOVE

(You can read this slowly yourself or have someone read it to you with some soft music in the background.)

Close your eyes for a moment and let come to your mind a picture or an image or a sensation that reminds you or feels like or brings back some memories of someone who changed your life in a positive, loving direction. You do not need to remember any specific instances; just get a feel for being in that person's presence. Just feel that and take it in. If a particular person does not come to mind, let yourself experience what it would be like to be on the receiving end of unconditional love. Imagine yourself getting warm in the new summer sunshine, feeling all the chill of winter melting away. That is what it is like. Feel all of those feelings that might be cold or restricting simply melting away. Give yourself the chance to feel that. Take it in as long as you like. You can repeat this experience whenever you want or whenever you feel the need. You will find it will become easier and easier to connect with this inner resource of unconditional love. Remember, "I have loved you with an everlasting love." (Jr 31:3 AKJ)

Hopefully, for each one of us there is a person in our lives who graced us with that sense of unconditional love, that total and complete acceptance. For me it was my Aunt Ann, my mother's sister, who gave me that gift.

I grew up as an only child, and as much as I enjoyed my solitude, I also wanted to be around kids my own age. I missed some of the excitement and energy that can come from a bigger family. My aunt had four children, and I was sandwiched in between the oldest and second-oldest daughters, Cathy and Mary. Since we lived only a couple of blocks apart, when my mother was working, I would usually be over at their house for lunch, and would stop over many times to walk the dog, to play, or for no reason at all. The home was chaotic at times, but my aunt always had time for me. I can remember many loving instances, but for me it was the overall feeling that came from her to me, that feeling of unconditional love. I knew she loved me, not because I was good, or her nephew, but simply because I was who I was. I will never forget that awareness of being loved for just me. Nor will I forget the many times of darkness, gloom, and despair which that sense of unconditional love has helped me get through.

We detach when we cease to concentrate on the object of our attachment and focus on the positive movement of God's grace flowing through us.

How do we detach with love? How do we let unconditional love work with us and flow through us? We detach when we cease to concentrate on the object of our attachment and focus on the positive movement of God's grace flowing through us. There is a wonderful story from the Buddhist tradition which expresses this ideal.

Every day, the little monk sits by the side of the road just outside of the village. People pass by and greet him and ask for his blessing, some drop offerings in the monk's begging bowl, others stop to talk of their problems and difficulties, or share their joys and gratitude, and occasionally someone might stop to ask for a solution to a particular vexing problem.

One day the richest man in the village came by and said, "Monk, I have a problem with greed; what can I do about it?" The monk smiled, took up his quill and a piece of rice paper, wrote down a few things, and handed the paper to the rich man. The man read the items on the paper and threw up his hands in impatience. "I have a problem with greed; these things you have asked me to do are not connected with greed at all." The little monk smiled and said, "If you continue to do these things you will no longer have a problem with greed."

On the paper was written: "Before you enter the village, drop a gold coin on the ground. When you enter town, go to the grocer and buy three days worth of food for one of the poorer families of your village, and have it delivered anonymously. Before you go home, buy gifts for your wife and children. When you enter your home greet your family with love and respect, and allow them to plan the evening," and so on.

Not to be overly simplistic, but detachment is not getting rid of something so much as it is changing the focus. Emmet Fox in his wonderful work *The Golden Key* suggests that whenever a problem arises, do not focus on the problem, but focus on God instead. Prayer is also a powerful means of detachment. What do we do in prayer? We shift our focus.

Putting the focus on myself is not self-centeredness; it is self-love. I change the focus from outside of me to inside. One way I can do that is by asking myself a simple question, especially if I am involved in a codependent kind of relationship, "What needs of mine have I been neglecting while I have been taking care of the other?" The question might not create change by itself, but the information will certainly heighten my awareness. I will be able to see choices and ways of being able to detach from whatever I need to let loose. I can realize, with love rather than anger, that I have been neglecting my real needs, be they physical, mental, emotional, or spiritual.

I also do not want to become lost or preoccupied with what I could have done or should have done, because as long as my energy is going in the direction of the past there is no way I am going to take care of myself well. By focusing on what I can do now to grow and heal, I will begin to lovingly nurture myself.

Letting go is not without its pain either, as we all know. Letting go has its own grieving. What is important for me to remember here is that the pain or discomfort I might feel is the pain of healing. It is like putting peroxide on a cut, or getting a deep massage on sore muscles. I can also know, as with all of life, this too will pass.

Letting go allows me the freedom to hold my life experiences differently. I can hold them as lessons rather than burdens. Right now, I might ask myself, "What can I turn around in my life? Where do I need to change my focus? Can I turn impatience into the energy of creation? Can I turn judgment of another into learning something about myself? Can I look at fear as a lack of love and work on loving more?" I begin to see a bigger picture. The choices are inside of me, nowhere else.

Many times I work with people who are diligently striving to let go, and they are working and working and praying and praying and nothing seems to happen. When this kind of stuckness happens to me, I need to keep in mind, "I can't push the river." I need to accept and love myself right where I am. Again, this acceptance is what opens me for transformation to occur. As my inner vision increases through practice, loving acceptance, awareness, and detachment provide even more of an atmosphere for me to grow. I become more aware of the choices in my life. I have a wider range of options. The world is no longer black and white and not just many shades of gray either, but multicolored and multi-faceted.

Whether we are talking about detaching from a person or a thing, the method of detachment is love and acceptance. In detaching from a thing, we do not hate or become entrenched in another negative feeling, which just forms more attachment. I deeply realize its uselessness to me now, and let go. I do not feed it with any emotion at all. I begin to feed more positive healing thoughts and feelings that are available to me. Detachment with a person involves loving acceptance of who, what, and where they are, without judgment, without attachment to unacceptable behaviors, and, at the same time, loving devotion to ourselves and our own healing.

Above all, detachment with love is total loving without judgment, expectations, or control.

MEDITATION: LOVING WITHOUT LIMITS

As you get comfortable, relaxed, and open, take
a few deep cleansing breaths, opening even more.

Count backwards from ten to one as you breathe deeply.
You can feel a sense of lightness and receptiveness as you allow Spirit
to speak to you, sharing with you exactly what you need.

Breathe deeply and experience yourself more and more relaxed as you
open to this meditation.

What is it like to be loved unconditionally?

What would it be like to love unconditionally?

Within all of us is the heart of unconditional love.

Breathe. Get in touch with your body, not just your physical body, but
the energy field you live in. Breathe into that energy and when you hear
the word "love" notice where it resonates within your awareness, and
now breathe into that place of resonance. Breathe into it, and now notice
the point of resonance with the words "unconditional love." Breathe into
that. Breathe into the essence of unconditional love within you.

Nothing need be forced, pushed, or analyzed, just breathe into that energy and let it flow. Let it begin to flow into every cell and fiber of your
being, physical, mental, emotional, and spiritual.

Pause...

You might experience the flow as warmth or lightness or whatever it is
you are experiencing.

Pause...

Relationships with God, others, and even ourselves require openness, honesty, and a willingness to grow.

We are all one, but before we realize that fully, we need to open ourselves to another. The realization of this deepest of truths, that we are all one, begins when we open ourselves to another.

As you travel inward, notice the yearning inside of you for intimacy. If you do not recognize it yet, just imagine what that yearning would feel like.

If you are already in a relationship, you might find your focus and your energy drawn to your partner. If not, then you can either imagine another person you love, or tune into the sensations of loving within yourself right now. Know that the desire to love is also love. Let the energy flow.

Notice how much you can learn from it. It can be hunger as well as peace; it can be joy as well as longing.

Begin to be conscious again of your breathing. Breathe deeply and stretch. Come fully back here in your body, completely centered and grounded.

Get up, stretch, and look around you. Become familiar with the place again, feeling yourself in your body. Journal or process any other way you like.

NUGGETS

The opposite of control is detachment and acceptance. Acceptance is embracing the responsibility for my own life, my own feelings, my own actions.

Control is a counterfeit for caring.

I can still want you to fix me even though I know you cannot.

Love never encourages negativity.

To love, to be open to love as fully as we can be, we need to be as empty and as unencumbered as possible.

Far from loving less or fostering indifference, true detachment allows me to love without limits.

What I am experiencing right now in my life are lessons that, in a mysterious way, I have attracted to myself. My life experiences are my learning. I have no right to interfere with the lessons you are learning and you have no right to interfere with mine. By saving someone from their pain we might be stopping them from learning. Pain is not the only way we learn, but it is sometimes a necessary process.

Detachment or letting go is a deep inner sense; you can even feel it physically in your body; you feel your guts unwind. That is one of the ways of knowing that detachment is taking place. Our bodies are tremendous barometers for this letting go. We cannot force the process to happen, but our bodies will help us know.

THE GRACE OF FORGIVENESS

SHORTLY AFTER *we were married, I did something that was upsetting to Margo. I cannot recall what it was. It might have been a misplaced phone message or my forgetting to do something I said I was going to do. What I do recall was that she was upset. I had no idea how to change that. I remember saying, "Well, I guess it's all over." She looked at me as if I was crazy. "I am upset now," she said, "and I soon will let go of it for good." She introduced me to the healing power of forgiveness.*

Forgiveness releases the toxic energy of anger and resentment which drains the inner self and creates imposing barriers to all relationships. Release heals me when I forgive and when I allow myself to be forgiven.

When I ask for forgiveness, I open my heart in compassion and allow myself to understand the hurt I might have caused others. Instead of shame and guilt, which are the ego's response to imperfection, I am lovingly humbled by recognizing my shortcomings, and open myself to grace and transformation.

When I open myself up to forgiveness from God or another, I recognize, in depth, that I am not what I do. My True Self and my actions are not the same thing. When I recognize that my actions are not who I am, I acknowledge this same truth in others. With that sublime recognition, I am more open to releasing my anger and resentment towards you. Thus forgiveness creates an infinite spiral ever reaching towards Oneness.

Forgiveness gives the freedom to live simply and in the present. The more stuff you are holding onto, the more complicated and burdensome life becomes. What are you holding onto that is holding you back? Is it fear, anger, resentment, or self-criticism? No matter what you are holding onto, the antidote, the release is forgiveness. Forgiveness is letting go; holding on or "un-forgiveness" creates a state of mind dominated by anger, fear, jealousy, guilt, and resentment. The negative results of this holding on are legion: all forms of self-destructive behavior, barriers to healthy relationships, physical illness, and a sense of isolation from God and others.

When we are holding on, we perceive ourselves and others as guilty and flawed. Our faith is eroded; we become vengeful and vindictive; we tend to focus on outside inconsequential values rather than the more important ones inside; we ignore or deny our feelings by suppression or projection onto others; we live in blame, shame, and guilt; we are fearful of looking at ourselves, and especially looking at ourselves lovingly.

I am stuck in judgmental thinking more than I would like to admit. Whenever I am holding onto anger, fear, jealousy, or hurt my judgmental mind kicks in reflexively. What do I do then? I have discovered that the antidote to judgment and all the baggage it creates is forgiveness. If I am holding on, everything I am holding onto is occupying the space that could be filled with love, grace, and peace. With forgiveness, I let go of my stuff and then God comes in and sweeps it up.

The Lord's Prayer directs us to know that we are forgiven "as we forgive." That is not a directive to God; it is the simple statement of a truth: we can only be forgiven as we forgive. Forgiveness means letting go, making a space, and opening up. If I am locked up and holding onto fear, anger, resentment, then there is little room for God to enter.

Jesus not only preached forgiveness, He also demonstrated it many times. Often He would say, "Thy sins are forgiven thee," even when a more physical miracle was expected. Forgiveness is the open door to love and compassion. Without forgiveness we remain self-centered, isolated, and trapped in our limited vision of ourselves and the world.

Not too long ago I heard, "When you forgive, everything will change." I thought, "How could anyone believe that? There must be more than that. Is it possible? Can it be that simple?"

I looked at all the anger, fear, and negative thoughts I had about myself. I examined all areas of my life: physical, mental, emotional, and spiritual. What would it be like if I were free of all that negativity?

My body is not in the kind of shape I would like it to be in. Of course I am sixty-five and probably will not have the body of a twenty year-old, but that's beside the point. I still have the idea that my body should be much more perfect than it is. I get colds and infections occasionally, and that should not be happening to me. I am short; I need glasses. I am angry at all my physical imperfections.

I am so grateful for my intellect; it is a marvelous tool and my mind has continued to serve me well as a teacher, counselor, writer, and many other areas of my life. It also can create limitations. My mind wanders. Outrageous thoughts occur to me. When I want to be quiet, my mind makes the most noise. When I want to stop trying to figure things out and just be in the mystery, my mind will not let go. My thoughts not only intrude on the present moment, they also create fear, anxiety, guilt, and remorse about the past or the future. I can be angry at my mind and my thoughts for not being as disciplined as I think they should be.

Sometimes I believe how I feel is who I am. Emotions are powerful influences and they can sometimes take over my life. It would be wonderful to be taken over by joyfulness and exuberance all the time, but I am one of those people (perhaps it is my Irish heritage) who leans towards the melancholy, depressed, and overwhelmed states of mind. I wish that were not true, but it is. I am angry at my emotional nature because it is not happy all the time.

When I look at my soul and my spiritual work, I realize I do not pray or meditate as much as I think I should. I do not identify with my soul and my spiritual nature as much as I would like. I think I am not as close to God as I would like to be; I think I should be better than I am. So I am angry at my soul for not being more assertive. I am angry with myself for not putting my soul first. The list can go on and on and on.

Then I thought, what would it be like if I forgave myself? What would it be like if I let go of all my negative feelings towards my body, mind, emotions, and spirit? What would happen? I would be free! Would any of the previously mentioned conditions change? Maybe, maybe not, but I would have changed. I would be like a balloon with its sandbags cut free, flying, unencumbered, and so much closer to the truth of who I really am, an unconditionally loved child of God.

Forgiveness allows me to be at peace; to be free of the past; to experience myself as strong and capable; to love and be loved.

Forgiveness allows me to be at peace, to be free of the past, to experience myself as strong and capable, to love and be loved. Forgiveness allows everything to be as it is. My relationship with God, others, and myself are open, loving, and unencumbered. In a state of forgiveness, my energy can now be directed in more positive, healthy ways for myself and others.

Forgiveness calls for deep levels of self-honesty and love. The energy that I put into surrender in the form of forgiveness allows me to honor, feel, and release all the many feelings that might be connected to my life experiences. Feelings such as rage, anger, shame, fear, and hurt are all very real. All these feelings need to be acknowledged, accepted, and dealt with in order for forgiveness to be lasting.

Many confuse forgiveness with being a victim. Forgiveness neither condones the act nor absolves the perpetrator. Forgiveness is about me, not the other person. When I release my anger and resentment and focus on my own well-being and healing, that is when I am free. As Thomas Merton beautifully stated, "The arrow with which I shoot my enemy has to pass through my own heart." When I drop my quiver with forgiveness, I no longer wound you and I no longer wound myself.

Forgiveness is similar to the process of grieving. It follows a pattern of willingness, evaluation, feeling, letting go, and opening to love.

WILLINGNESS

I need to be willing to release my anger, fear, and grudges, but sometimes I am just not at that place. I know I need to be willing, but I also need to remember that if I am not at the point of willingness yet, I need to be willing to be willing. I need to take a step or a few steps back. I do not concentrate on where I am not; I concentrate on where I am. If I am not at the stage of complete willingness, then I embrace myself where I am and allow myself to be open to the grace of moving forward. I need to realize there must be a part of me that is willing to let go or I would not be examining the issue at all.

Go to the place inside of you that is willing to be willing. That is where you start. You are willing to be willing to forgive. Say that to yourself, "I am willing to be willing to forgive." "I am taking care of my feelings; I am embracing myself where I am now. I am willing to be willing." There will be times in your life when you are not ready to let go, when you continue to hold on. That is just where you are at the moment. The realization is not a call for self-judgment, but for self-awareness. You hold on as long as you need to hold on, and when you are ready to let go you are ready to let go.

When you feel the feelings and open to the willingness of forgiveness, you can begin to realize this process is not about the other person or the event; it is about you. Your forgiveness and letting go are about *your* anger and resentment, however justified they might be.

In your letting go you acknowledge that your anger and resentment are not affecting the person you are angry with, but your holding on is killing you.

EVALUATION

There are events in my life which have produced genuine wounds and others that have simply bruised my ego. The former need the surrender work of forgiveness; the latter, I just need to let go of.

Most occurrences in life are not about me at all. If I could just realize that truth, life would be much gentler and simpler. I find myself waiting in line, in the middle of a traffic jam, thinking someone is being rude to me–those are some of the many things that have nothing to do with me. Nobody is doing anything to me. Although I am prone to anger and impatience in those situations there is nothing to do except to let it go.

How important is this? So I let him get to the red light ahead of me. So she didn't write the check before she got into the checkout lane. What difference is that going to make to me today, tomorrow, or next week? I discover what a useless waste of energy it is to dwell on any of that, and how utterly self-centered it is to think any of that was about me.

When we are identified with our ego we can perceive practically anything as an affront. Jacquie Small once suggested we make a distinction between "ego hurts" and "heart hurts." We need to develop an honest, healthy awareness of ourselves to make this distinction.

Ego hurts arise from everyday circumstances, and have no real effect on anything important. In fact, most ego hurts occur in the mind rather than the external world. I might think someone has looked at me funny, or they didn't say "Thank you" when I held the door for them, or they didn't compliment me the way I thought they ought to. My list of perceived wrongs done to me is endless, and I need to differentiate between those events, real or imagined, and those which truly require my forgiveness. There will be many ego hurts that I simply need to let go of. I will own them, accept them as my reaction to my ego's limited view of things, and I will move on.

Heart hurts are those events that we feel have truly damaged us: if we experience ourselves as victimized by someone else's anger, especially if we were abused or treated unjustly, if we were physically harmed, or if our emotions were discounted or ignored. These are issues which require our attention. We forgive; we let go so that we can heal. As we listen to our heart we can know what is significant and what is not. We will neither hold onto the meaningless and trivial complaints of the ego, nor will we discount events which wound us and drain us of power.

In forgiveness, we first let go of the issues and incidents the ego has placed such importance on, and then we work through the process to let go and heal those issues and incidents which have hurt or wounded us. Both levels of surrender allow our soul's energy to foster healing and wholeness.

As with grieving, the process of forgiveness cannot be rushed. The surrender occurs at its own time. We do the conscious work, giving our soul the time and the space to let go.

FEELING

I have worked with people who have attempted to rush their forgiveness. They have been willing to forgive, but they have not yet done the necessary work with their feelings. If I attempt to forgive before I have dealt with my emotions, then I am left with feelings about myself that are neither good nor healthy. Many times if I try to forgive without feeling the anger and the other feelings I need to feel, I can be left with a sensation of incompleteness. That vacuum of incompleteness attracts all sorts of unhealthy ideas such as, "Well, maybe I did something to provoke this. Maybe it is my fault after all." No one deserves to be abused or mistreated in any way; however, in the wake of rushed forgiveness, I can be left with feelings of doubt and shame.

We have all heard the message, "Well, you just need to forgive," and we have attempted to put it into practice. Most of the time, however, what we end up doing is to push down or deny our feelings. Obviously, this is not healthy. Denial and repression are defense mechanisms, but they are not tools that allow for healing. What these defenses do is to protect us from our feelings for a time. Sometimes, protection is just what we need. Our defenses might allow us a time of numbness so that we can survive the trauma of whatever has been done to us. Then there comes a time when all of these feelings need to be dealt with in order for us to regain our mental and emotional health.

When I rush this process of forgiveness, I attempt to deal with all of these emotions of hurt, anger, and fear too quickly. In true and healthy forgiveness, I feel all the feelings, accept them, own them, let them move through me, and finally let them go.

The feelings which need attention in the process of forgiveness will vary from person to person and incident to incident, but the two dominant ones are anger and hurt.

I learned many erroneous ideas about anger growing up. As I began to understand how much of a role this emotion plays in both grieving and forgiveness, I knew I was going to need some work with this emotion of anger.

As I said earlier, I grew up in an alcoholic home; needless to say, there was a lot of anger floating around. Anger was sometimes explosive, usually out of proportion to the event, and always unpredictable and hurtful. More than anything else I learned that anger was a tool that was used to wound and manipulate. Anger was also like nuclear waste; it had a half-life of about fifty thousand years. It never went away. No matter what kinds of promises were made about "never bringing this up again," I knew that was a lie. Whatever the issue, it would always surface again as a weapon to hurt and control. It is not surprising that I spent much of my life denying and suppressing my anger.

Anger is a feeling with quite a bit of physical energy. Probably one of the first things that I need to do with anger is to discharge the physical energy connected with it. Yelling, screaming, pounding pillows–all are common ways of dealing with the physical aspects of anger.

Exercise and other forms of movement can also be very helpful. These methods are simply ways of releasing the physical side of the anger. What that does, from my experience, is give people the opportunity to look at and deal with the feeling of anger and all of the other feelings that might underlie the anger.

Dealing with the anger itself is another issue. Here I might really need some professional help in order to be able to understand and work with the feeling. Many times anger covers other feelings such as guilt, shame, fear, and hurt. These underlying feelings need to be dealt with also. When we have experienced the hurt of trauma, we need to find ways of honoring and dealing with all the resultant feelings. Certainly, finding a good therapist can be helpful. Someone I can really trust and talk to. Trust your gut with this one. In therapy, as well as in many areas of life, "One size does not fit everyone."

Friends who are understanding and supportive are a powerful and positive resource. There are also good self-help groups where I can get the support of a group and be helped and supported by some of the individuals in the group.

After I have released and dealt with my feelings of anger, hurt, and any others, that is when it is time to forgive. In fact, when I have dealt with all of those feelings, I might find that forgiveness has already happened.

Forgiveness is not about the other person; forgiveness is about me. I am the one who needs to forgive. I need to forgive, not because it is something that I have to do, but because it is something that will free me and free my energies to do more positive work for myself. I can claim my power and let myself and the world know I am no longer a victim. Now I have even more choices than I had before. Forgiveness is a way of unburdening myself, a way of freeing myself.

How do I forgive others? I stop punishing either outrightly or passive-aggressively. It is only when I stop punishing and let go that I can be open to love and loving. As long as my energies are devoted to punishing, they cannot be devoted to loving. Feelings directed towards a person or object can be either expansive or constrictive, not both.

Forgiveness is freedom. When I let go of anger, resentment, and judgment I am free. When I forgive myself I am free. When I allow myself to be forgiven by God and by others I am free. When I open myself to asking for forgiveness I am free.

LEARNING, FILLING UP, AND HEALING

Along with willingness, evaluation, and release of feelings, there is a finalizing stage of forgiveness called the learning or healing stage. It is the time when the space inside which has been emptied of punishment, guilt, fear, anger, and resentment is now filled with love, light, understanding. Jesus shared a parable about a person who was cleansed of a demon. He likened that person to a house that was cleaned up and aired out, but then seven other demons moved in worse than the first. (Mt 12:43-45) What happened? Nothing happened, and that was the problem. The person let go and was released of his demon, but did not fill in the empty space with anything. It is true that nature abhors a vacuum. When the space is freed inside of us we need to actively fill it with the good. We pray; we open ourselves to light and healing; we cultivate nurturing thoughts and ideas. We fill ourselves with all things good so that the goodness, light, and peace that we have received can flow through us, continuing our own healing and the healing of the world.

The power of living in the grace of forgiveness extends beyond my practice of forgiving another. In the realm of forgiveness there is also self-forgiveness–asking and accepting the forgiveness of others and accepting the forgiveness of God.

Just as I need to forgive others, I also need to forgive myself. Self-forgiveness, like all the other forms of forgiveness, is about letting go. This self-forgiveness is a lesson in how to deal with the self in a non-judgmental way that helps me to forgive others. I shudder when I imagine what it would be like if I spoke to other people the way I speak to myself.

Self-forgiveness is letting go of my own blame, shame, and guilt. It is the use of love rather than guilt to control or transform my actions. It is the letting go of the notion that mistakes make me awful or diminish me. Self-forgiveness is opening myself up to the love that I am.

Self-forgiveness allows me to deal with the issues at hand, even serious life occurrences such as sickness or loss. Rather than wasting all my energy on self-recrimination, I surrender and allow grace to lead and heal me.

If I get sick or am in trouble I do not beat myself up. I do not want to get into the useless thinking that I must have done something wrong to deserve this or that I somehow created this situation. Even if my thinking did play a role, being angry at myself does nothing to create a solution.

If a friend or a loved one became sick or found themselves in difficult financial straits would I say, "Oh, you're sick. Well, I wonder what you did to create that?" No. I would be immediately searching for a way to comfort the one who is ill as well as finding a solution to the problem. If I can do that for another, I need to work on doing that for myself.

I have used guilt to attempt to create better behaviors. The fact that it never works eludes me when I am working out of my ego-consciousness. Guilt serves a purpose for about thirty seconds. Guilt is a method I have invented to try and stop myself from doing some of those old unacceptable behaviors. I think to myself, "If I feel bad enough about the past, then I will be good now."

Along with seeing the woundedness, self-forgiveness allows me to see the love in myself as well. I let go of blame, shame, and guilt. If I can begin to see the love in myself, I can begin to see the love in you.

I have been thoughtless, mean, indifferent, and uncaring. Even though I have not been that way deliberately, I have still been offensive and wounding. I need to ask for forgiveness.

There is a huge difference between saying "I'm sorry" and asking for forgiveness. "I'm sorry" simply says, "I feel bad because I made you feel bad." In that scene, it is my own feelings I am more concerned about. Notice how subtle the ego can be. Even when I am attempting to repair hurt feelings I might have contributed to in you,

I still make it about me.

Forgiveness happens when I open my heart to the sense of the hurt I caused another, and open myself to their love, and then I am willing to continue to hold them in an open heart even if they do not reciprocate. Do you feel the work in that?

Then there is the mystery of accepting God's forgiveness. Rather than looking at myself as a sinner, that I am dreadful or there is something wrong with me, I would prefer to think that my mistakes come from acting out of my limited ego-consciousness. This limited consciousness cuts me off from the love that is my birthright. Accepting God's forgiveness is not self-judgment; it is opening myself to the love that is already there.

How many times have I heard this one: "I know God forgives me, but I cannot forgive myself." That is baloney! If you truly accept God's forgiveness, you have to be forgiving of yourself as well.

As with the forgiveness of another this is not a blank check. It is more the recognition that we are at peace with the universe, that we are letting go and moving on. Forgiveness reminds us that we are open to the spiritual power of love rather than fear, grace rather than guilt, and peace rather than conflict.

The Old Testament is filled with images of an angry and vengeful God, yet amidst all the noise and fury is a most consoling allusion about forgiveness, "Though your sins be as red as scarlet, they shall be as white as snow." (Is 1:18 NSRV)

MEDITATION: FORGIVENESS

As you get comfortable, relaxed, and open,
take a few deep cleansing breaths,
opening even more.

Count backwards from ten to one as you breathe
deeply. You can feel a sense of lightness and receptiveness as you allow
Spirit to speak to you, sharing with you exactly what you need.

Breathe deeply and experience yourself more and more relaxed as you open to this meditation.

Let forgiveness in; this is where it begins.

How burdened we are at times with anger, fear, and resentment. How often we feel things, even things long past, over and over again such as past hurts and jealousies.

Let go of body, mind, and emotions. Let go of thoughts, doubts, fears, guilt, and shame.

Pause...

If there is any negativity hanging around, bring it to the altar. Come bring yourself as you are at this minute with as little judgment as you can.

Bring yourself and all your thoughts and feelings, your past and future, your body and your mind; bring it all to the altar.

Let your prayer be, "Here is how I see myself. This is the baggage I carry. I know I am more than this. I know You love me more than I love myself and for this and so much more I am grateful. I come now with all my stuff even though I know most of it is a reflection of my guilt and fear. I come to the altar to be healed, to be forgiven. I consciously offer You my fear, my guilt, my sadness. I come to You with the desire to be whole, to know Your Truth within me, to know that I am one with You, to know that I am already forgiven, that in Your Mind there was nothing to forgive. I open myself to the consciousness of forgiveness, peace, compassion. May I love as You love; may I know that love is who I am.

Thank you, God. Amen."

Begin to be conscious again of your breathing. Breathe deeply and stretch. Come fully back here in your body, completely centered and grounded.

Get up, stretch, and look around you. Become familiar with the place again, feeling yourself in your body. Journal or process any other way you like.

NUGGETS

Forgiving is *not* about other people, or running away from feelings, or denying them, or saying what happened is OK, or being a doormat.

Forgiveness is neither a feeling nor a moral judgment.

If you have not realized it yet, forgiveness is about surrender.

Forgiveness is acknowledging our wounds and opening to healing.

We have a yearning for forgiveness; nurture the yearning.

There is a wise, considerate, loving voice inside of you. Listen to the voice that will validate you. Listen to your heart. Do not let feelings of fear or guilt pull you away from your heart.

If forgiveness is difficult, focus on your healing.

I am not my woundedness.

Forgive the person, not the act.

Less baggage, more flow.

Forgiveness is an act of will, willingness.

In the light of God's Love, which we comprehend more deeply with forgiveness, the baggage begins to evaporate.

Forgiveness is not something we do so much as what we let go of.

Forgiveness is also about treating myself with respect and love.

There is no such thing as forgiving and forgetting. Forgiveness does not mean forgetting. I will probably always have the memories with me. Forgiveness is about holding these memories in a different way.

Forgiveness is letting go of taking things personally.

Forgiveness is another way of looking at surrender. Forgiveness is letting go of something that no longer serves me. Forgiveness is also a way of entering into the path of non-judgment and non-attachment.

Nothing of importance can be taken away from me.

For most of us, we realize that those we need to forgive have done things to us that are terrible. They have hurt us deeply; the hurts that have been done to us have affected our entire lives and many times affected our relationships with other people as well. This is especially true with issues of sexual abuse.

I do not know if I can say that sexual abuse or any other crime is unforgivable. I simply do not know. This to me is a moral distinction and a very individual one. It does seem to me that if I make anything unforgivable, then I have lost some choices for myself, and I have limited myself.

Forgiveness is a powerful demonstration of love.

Sometimes, especially if we are working through abuse trauma, we can give our power away to another, even a therapist. I encourage people to trust their guts, and even if they have worked with someone for some time and do not feel comfortable or safe with them, it might be time to make a change.

There is nothing wrong with us if we do not forgive; we are just not ready.

Forgiveness is always a difficult issue to perceive. In some ways it is very subtle, and in other ways it is very much out front. Most of us have the notion that forgiveness means doing something. To me, forgiveness is more about letting go than anything else.

A Course in Miracles states, "God cannot heal what we are not willing to let go of."

LETTING GO OF JUDGMENT

I STOPPED AND *imagined how uncluttered my mind would be if I were no longer carrying the energy-draining baggage of judgments, self-criticism, and useless internal dialogues. "Well, I wish I had been aware enough to do such and such. When she said that then I should have said this. That was such a stupid thing for me to say! What a jerk I am. I wonder what they are thinking of me now?" I have conversations like that all the time, not only with myself, but with all the other people I have living in my head. What if I simply let go and forgave myself? I imagined what it would be like to be free of all that useless chatter and clutter.*

Forgiveness creates the space for healing. When forgiveness is necessary, we realize we have fallen short of the mark that unconditional love sets for us. We have opted for protection rather than love, and we realize we have caused unnecessary pain to ourselves and others.

So often the necessity for forgiveness arises from the clinging machinations of my judgmental mind. There would be no need for forgiveness if my focus were directed towards loving myself and others.

My thinking mind is always making judgments; that is how it operates. To be in the space of non-judgment, I must be aware when the mortal mind is trying to run the show. I can know that the intellect is a marvelous tool, but it is also a limited instrument.

When my soul and intuitive heart-mind are in charge, my attention is fixed on what I need to do, with God's help, to grow and transform. When I am open to this grace, and I consciously know I can change no one but myself, I am on the path of non-judgment. Non-judgment not only prevents the hurt and pain caused by self-centeredness, it also focuses on reaching the mark of unconditional love rather than missing it. When I do not judge, when I allow the power of God to lead me in love, I am free. Surrender is letting go of judgment; surrender is being in the space of non-judgment.

Since we continually need to evaluate life situations and make decisions about them, what do we do? Do we simply approach life passively? If we are not supposed to judge, does that mean we never assess, evaluate, or act? The quality of non-judgment is not opposed to necessary decision making. In fact, one of the gifts of the Holy Spirit is discernment. Suspending judgment, or leaving judgment up to God, is not the same as never making a decision. We all need to make decisions about situations that come down on us in life. Even the present moment demands choices. The key issue is, who is doing the leading, the Holy Spirit or my fearful ego?

How can I tell the difference between discernment, a gift of the Spirit, and judgment, which comes from ego? Judgment will always produce a sense of separation. Judgment is about identification with our story or the story we made up about someone else. When we listen, in the quiet, to the wee small voice within, we can all recognize the difference between the flow of honest discernment and the stagnation of judgment. Prayer, meditation, and the practice of the presence of God are essential elements in being open to the voice of Spirit. It is up to each one of us to put the distinction into practice. Discernment will always lead me in the way of the open heart. Judgment will always close it.

When presented with a course of action, the key questions are, "Does what I am planning open my heart or close it? Does my action open me to the source of love or close me off from it?"Answering those questions requires continuing practice and awareness. The answers my heart gives me might not always be logical or certain on an intellectual level, but they will always resonate with the Truth of God within me.

My practice could be as simple as choosing to alter my language. I recall an experiment that Leo Buscaglia, who was called the Love Doctor, did years ago in one of his classes. He covered two walls of his classroom with heavy paper and had the class write all of the negative words they could think of on one wall. It was covered with all the expected profanities, along with words such as hate, fear, and hopelessness. On the opposite wall, he asked them to write all the positive words they could think of. Again, there were the many words we might except, such as love, kindness, nice, cute, along with other words such as giving, openness, and simplicity.

The class assignment for the next month or so directed everyone to monitor their speech both in and outside the classroom. The students were asked to use only the words on the positive wall, and to avoid the ones on the negative wall. The results were amazing. Everyone reported a significant and positive change in attitude that was consistent with a simple change in vocabulary. A huge shift in consciousness and focus took place just by changing the words they used.

Have ever noticed yourself going through a good day in your life, feeling peaceful and content and thinking everything is together and cool? Then you make a judgment, "Oh, look at that stupid so-and-so." As soon as you make that judgment, you can physically feel your heart close down. Your heart closes off, your blood pressure goes up, and your world shrinks to encompass only you and your judgment. In reality, it is not even all of you; it is just your ego. That contracted space is a pretty lonely and uncomfortable place to be.

When my focus is lovingly on myself, even when I realize I have made a mistake or an error in thinking, I do not have to be judgmental.

The recognition is simply an awareness that can allow me to transform and grow. The positive awareness of an error leads me to ask, "How can I do this differently? How can I open my heart rather than close it?" Judgment comes about when I make myself wrong, bad, guilty, or shamed. When I become attached to these negative emotions my energy changes from the positive energy of transformation to the negative energy of stuckness and depression.

A few months ago, while I was changing baby Fionn's (our youngest grandchild) diaper, I became distracted in helping his four year old sister. Before I could react, Fionn rolled off the couch to the floor and began to cry. I was frightened, guilty, and devastated at causing pain to this little one. I was immediately flooded with thoughts of what an awful person I was, images of rushing him to the hospital, and imagining the angry, accusing voices of his parents.

I held him and wept. I think I was crying more than he was. He was fine, no bumps or bruises. Then I realized I had become so wrapped up in my own feelings of pain and guilt that I was ignoring the two little ones that needed me most at that moment. Judgment directed towards myself was preventing me from loving. My choice was either to stay in self-judgment and self-punishment or to get back to loving those in my charge. After some struggle, I chose the latter.

I carry that event with me today, not as guilt, but as a reminder of how dear those children are to me, and how easily my attachment to judgment can take me away from those I love the most.

As judgment occurs, we put someone or something in a box or a category. Whenever we put a label on someone, we have reduced the person to a thing, a controllable object. We have taken a complex human being and made him into a very simplistic idea. "Oh, he's Irish. She's a Catholic. They live in the south end of town. He's a lawyer." Then all the prejudices and other judgments we have collected over the years become attached to that label. The person becomes a thing, a label, a box, an object.

Through judgment, I also decide the meaning and motivation behind other people's actions. All I have to do is think about how ridiculous that is. I have a difficult enough time understanding why I do the things I do! What makes me think I am going to have a clear picture of what motivates another? Judgment takes us out of ourselves and into other people's stuff which is none of our business.

The driver who speeds by me could be rushing home to a sick child. I immediately make a judgment that he/she is an idiot for going so fast. If I am honest with myself I realize that I am not angry at them for going too fast; I am not thinking that their speed is putting me in danger. What I am angry at is their arrogance in passing me! My judgment is about something I have taken as a personal affront, and it is all ego. Even if the person might be rushing home to a six-pack; six-pack or sick child, either way, it is none of my business.

The saddest outcome of the process of judgment is that all the energy of judgment and the ensuing anger and negative feelings that are generated is wasted energy. My judgment does nothing to transform me, it only brings me down. In the end it leaves me with less resources and reserves than I had before.

Every time I make a judgment, I move from a place of infinite love, understanding, and compassion to a tight, confining, black hole that I have created for myself. It sucks the life out of me. When I am judging myself or another, there is no room for compassion, gratitude, or forgiveness. All of my energies are eaten up by jealousy, envy, shame, and "not-enoughness."

Scripture abounds in counsel with regard to judgment. "Judge not and you shall not be judged." "Do not focus on the grain of sand in your brother's eye. Remove the beam from your own eye first." (Lk 6:37 & 42) We are continually encouraged to put the focus on ourselves, not as judgment, but as awareness.

The more aware we become of our ego's defensiveness and its continual need to protect itself, the more we can gently stop the process of judgment. When we extend ourselves beyond the ego's limited consciousness our energies are directed away from judgment and towards our own awareness and growth.

As soon as I become aware I am in the throes of judgment, I want to immediately shine the light inwards. I want to begin to discover what is going on inside of me that is creating the need for judgment. Is it jealousy, anger, or fear? As I begin to uncover the source of my need to judge, I want to be careful not to turn my awareness into self-judgment. That would be such an easy subtle trap to fall into. Rather than self-judgment, I want to realize my feelings of hurt, jealousy, or anger are emanating from a wounded part of me which is asking to be healed. My work is that of healing, not judging.

Many spiritual teachers suggest that it is our sense of separation which is the most harmful misconception under which we can labor. Any form of judgment–which is always, ultimately, self-judgment, alienates us from our Source, our own soul, and all our brothers and sisters. Judgment, in any form, undeniably reinforces that sense of separation.

We live in a culture of separateness. We are surrounded by judgments and comparisons. It is fascinating to me that we have created a culture and economy that only exists by producing a continual sense of inadequacy. Advertising, for example, not only creates an unnecessary need, but also creates comparisons and standards that none of us can live up to. Most judgments, especially about externals, are absolutely ridiculous. They are not rooted in any truth at all. These external standards are based on fabricated social norms that are whimsical at best. There are no lasting criteria for external values. What was beautiful at one time is commonplace the next. Unfortunately, some of us center our whole world and our image of ourselves on this kind of false information of fickle, useless, and, ultimately, meaningless judgments.

I love watching babies. I know there are some things they naturally like and some things they do not, but I also think many likes and dislikes are learned rather than innate. For a baby, the smell of poop can be just as interesting as the smell of a flower. There are no good smells or bad smells; in some ways all of them are good because they are interesting. It is only later on that I begin to learn that one is good and another is bad, according to someone else's standards.

The Gospel message of Jesus is continually leading us beyond appearance. There are the ongoing admonitions to the Scribes and the Pharisees about being too wrapped up in externals and missing the essence of things. The parable of the Prodigal Son illustrates both sons lost in delusion and holding onto values which are fickle at best. Jesus deliberately associated with whores and tax collectors. The "first shall be last," He said. "Even Solomon in all his glory" was not as splendid as a flower growing in a field. (Lk 13:30 & 12:27)

If judgment produces a sense of separation, then letting go of judgment and focusing on creating an atmosphere of love and compassion produces a sense of unity and cohesion. If judgment leads to separation, then focusing on our Oneness would be a practical way to avoid judgment and the chaos and energy drain it produces. I can approach life by thinking, "What's wrong with you or me?" or I can ask, "What can I do to enhance our sense of unity and Oneness?"

The subtle yet profound implication surrounding non-judgment is that we are all so much the same. Of course our life circumstances differ, but we all have our roles we play; we all have hurts, fears, doubts. We all have wounds to heal, but beneath and through all of that, we all desire peace, freedom, and a sense of belonging. Everyone's actions are geared towards these goals.

When we remove ourselves from the strictures of judgment, we are now free to be loving and compassionate both to ourselves and others.

A few years ago, I was asked to give a weekend retreat for the music ministers of a local parish. I was doing a lot of that kind of work back then so I immediately said "Yes," then had my usual wrestling match with my doubts and insecurities. "I'm not good enough to do this." "What if they don't like me?" "I don't have enough material." "I should have said, 'No'; what was I thinking?" It is an internal drill I am very familiar with. I caged the gremlins for awhile and put together a prayerful, thoughtful workshop that would cover Friday night and all day Saturday.

I am severely directionally challenged, so whenever I am travelling to a new place, I give myself plenty of time. (Today I am eternally grateful for my GPS!) I got lost a few times, but still managed to arrive a little early. The group was just cleaning up after dinner. I quickly introduced myself, and found a comfortable spot in the living room which would be our primary setting for the workshop.

As I sat there, I could not help but hear the overlapping conversations from the kitchen. I became aware that besides being musicians these people were also highly educated professionals. More and more, I began to feel myself to be the inadequate outsider; and I experienced myself becoming tinier and more insignificant as I sank more deeply into that plush living room chair.

Even though I had been through this mental mine-field before, my many excursions into self-destructive thinking did not make this particular journey less dangerous, less meaningful, or less hurtful. I even started to think of some excuses to leave. Before I could formulate a workable escape plan, everyone trooped into the room, laughing, joking, and teasing. They appeared happy and free; I was miserable and trapped.

I introduced myself to the group, began with a prayer, and then on inspiration suggested, "Why don't we all take a moment of quiet to notice what is going on with us, and then we will take some time to share where we are in our lives right now." The atmosphere immediately changed from one of frivolity to quiet. It was not heavy, just thoughtful. I almost felt guilty for popping the balloon. As everyone shared, I began to see beyond the appearances which had trapped my ego in judgment and comparison.

Their sharing was not complicated stuff, but it was all from the heart. There was sadness concerning relationships with parents or siblings who did not seem as if they would ever change. There were unique moments of joy describing children and moments of the power of creation in music or song. There were moments of self-doubt and fear. There was the helplessness that comes from knowing someone we love is in pain and we cannot do anything about it. There were nightmares and hope, loneliness and laughter.

I remember one woman describing looking out her bedroom window with her cat that morning. A bird happened to fly very close to them, and the cat struck out reflexively, killing the bird. She said there was very little blood, and the bird was still warm as she picked it up, wishing it were not dead. She cried as she described all the paradoxical feelings–the beauty of the bird, the seeming cruelty of the cat, the poignancy of her cat's split second reflex that was so perfect and so deadly. None of us could have explained what the tears were all about, but we all knew; we all connected to the naturalness, beauty, sadness of it all. The outpouring of grief, sadness, worry, joy, doubt, and gratitude was tremendously moving to me. It made me realize that underneath it all we are so much alike.

I took a deep breath. It was OK; I was home. They are just like me. Our outsides might be different, but our insides are quite the same.

Our life circumstances are unique, but everyone I have ever met has experienced a substantial amount of life's pain. The major thought which increases our pain is we think we are alone in our experience. Our perspective and our level of judgment would change immensely if we took a moment to realize the person in front of us, behind us, beside us, and the person who just bumped into us has experienced as much suffering as we have. In fact, the reason that person just bumped into us is because they were preoccupied with their own pain. How does that realization change our view of things?

Letting go of judgment allows you to go beyond the boundaries of externals. Non-judgment makes the inside of you the truth rather than the outside. You can go beyond all those old pieces of identity that you might cling to–your roles, your feelings, your pain, your grief, even those things that bring you joy. Those feelings and situations remain important, but they do not need to define your life. No externals need to define your life. The essence of joy, love, peace, abundance, and all the other attributes of God are within you. Nothing can really bring you joy; the joy is within you.

As I become more focused on my inner truth, the truth of Oneness, I do not need to deny or ignore the external world. My body is real on a physical level, but it is not who I am. I am creating the illusion of separateness when I make my body, my mind, my emotions, my past, my future, my wealth, or any other external element identical to who I am. When I identify another person with any

of these external labels, I do not really see them either; I am just seeing the "clothes" they wear.

When I say "I see the Christ in you," I don't mean I see the Christ
in Margo, or Susan, or Jack. I am not speaking about the personal
"you." I see past your body and the roles you play. I see beyond
appearances and all the "clothes" you wear. The You that I see as
Christ is your essence, your Godliness, which is the same as mine.
As one of my teachers states, "If we were to strip off all the trap-
pings there would only be one of us here."

Michelangelo is often quoted as saying that all he needed to do to
create his statue of David was to cut away all that was not David. It
is a beautiful truth. The essence of who we are is already here. Our
job is to release all that is not the truth. What we forget is that it took
Michelangelo more than just one whack of the hammer to allow
David to reveal itself.

It doesn't require any work at all to become one with God
because that is already true; what requires work is letting go of the
stuff of judgment. It is work to clean out all the thoughts we hold
that still scream separateness. The work of letting go of judgment
and comparison is continuous. As with all of the steps on the path of
Spirit, becoming aware of our Oneness with God requires that we
are open to our intuition and listen to God's wisdom speaking in and
through us. We listen to our deep truth, God's truth, and we remain
teachable. We remain open to deeper knowing.

Let us be teachable, let us learn, let us love, let us say, "God,
please enter my heart where you already live. Let me know who I
am beyond the pain, beyond the suffering, beyond the loss, and
beyond the emptiness. Let me know who I am without judgment and
let me see You everywhere, in everyone, and everything, especially
when I look in the mirror. Amen."

MEDITATION: NON-JUDGMENT

As you get comfortable, relaxed, and open,
take a few deep cleansing breaths, opening even more.

Count backwards from ten to one as you breathe deeply.
You can feel a sense of lightness and receptiveness as you allow Spirit
to speak to you, sharing with you exactly what you need.

Breathe deeply and experience yourself more and more relaxed as you
open to this meditation.

When has judgment ever created peace, or even a positive solution?

Imagine yourself in a small private movie theater. You are all by yourself
and you find a comfortable chair to relax in. As the movie begins, you
notice you are the star, and the movie shows you walking through a typical
day in your life, at home, or school, or work. Keep a little distance
between yourself in the chair and the "you" on the screen. Notice how
quickly and easily the person on the screen forms judgments about
practically anything. There can be complex and personal judgments
such as, "Who does he think he is?" or "That was an awful thing to say.
I would never do something like that." There can be trivial ones as well
such as, "That piece of paper is too small." or "What an ugly-looking
chair." The mind goes on and on.

Notice how the judgments pile up and how at the end of the day you
seem like just one huge heap of judgments. There is not much room for
anyone or anything else.

Now imagine yourself at a moment in your life when you are at peace,
happy and free, just being in the moment. Here you are happy and free,
and then the phone rings or someone bumps into you. What happens to
your happiness and freedom?

Where did it go? What would allow you to return to that peaceful state of mind?

Pause…

Open to peacefulness.

Begin to be conscious again of your breathing. Breathe deeply and stretch. Come fully back here in your body, completely centered and grounded.

Get up, stretch, and look around you. Become familiar with the place again, feeling yourself in your body. Journal or process any other way you like.

NUGGETS

I have noticed when my language leans towards the profane, there is a backlog of feelings I have not taken care of. Anger seems to be the first emotion to surface, but usually underneath that are the more vulnerable feelings of hurt or fear. Negative language is like a warning sign to me that I am neglecting some important emotional needs. If I delve more deeply, I will discover most of my negativity is coming from self-judgment.

I can change no one but myself.

Judgment of another, or self–and its first cousin, comparison, is unproductive at best, destructive at worst.

How many classes have we sat in thinking, "Everybody is getting this but me."

We suffer from what is sometimes referred to as "terminal uniqueness."

To paraphrase Buddha: "Don't believe anything I tell you. Don't believe anything anyone tells you. Listen only to what resonates in your own heart."

It can be a paradoxical place where we know, and know that we know, and know that we do not know everything.

We judge ourselves so severely. We might not think we judge others so harshly, yet how can we not? If nothing else, the separation we have created with our judgment creates pain for us as well as those who love us.

The beautiful Zen poem the *Hsin-Hisn Ming* begins by stating, "The Great Way is not difficult for those who have no opinions. When love and hate are both absent, everything becomes clear and undisguised. Make one distinction, however, and heaven and earth are set infinitely apart."

So much of our energies are directed towards the behavior of others.

How silly to think an action will mean the same thing to us as it does to another. Even more outrageous is to think I can know another's motivation.

One of the challenges of the spiritual life is to go beyond appearances. To live in the Spirit is to focus on God and the attributes of God rather than getting sucked into the illusion and glamour of the world. Our spiritual awareness guides us to let go of our judgment of ourselves if we happen to stray from the path. The soul knows that guilt is not a motivator. Simply put, when you become aware you are off the path, get back on.

Creating a space for the release of judgment is an active process. Instead of directing energy to judgment, justified anger, prejudice, and self-righteousness, we now direct it towards personal examination and growth. When we are not wasting energy on judging ourselves or others with blame, shame, and guilt then we are free. We are not creating any baggage for ourselves or those around us. We are free and we free others as well from the grip of judgment, anger, and guilt.

LIVING IN THE MYSTERY

HOW I STRUGGLE *to know, to file everything away into nice, neat categories, yet at the same time I realize I would be terribly bored if the stuff of life were so neatly packaged. My intellect is a marvelous tool, but it does not fathom mystery. The intellect is not the mind of God; it is the mind of man. It is limited; it can know, but it is not even close to all-knowing.*

The refrain of an old Dylan song laments, "Ah, but I was so much older then, I'm younger than that now." Back when I was older, someone told me, "I love you." My mind responded in typical fashion by asking, "What does that mean?" The intellect always wants to find out what something means, but I know there are some aspects of life that go beyond explanation. The most important things in life cannot be explained. Can I explain love? Can I explain the unconditional love of God? Can I explain the workings of grace in my life? Can I explain the infinite sweetness in a baby's eyes? Do I have to?

While we were on a trip to Italy, Margo and I had the opportunity to visit the Sistine Chapel. It is truly an awe-inspiring place. When I entered, my eyes immediately went to the ceiling to find that piece of creation art depicting God reaching out to Adam. As magnificent as that scene was, I immediately became aware that the creation piece was only one of seven huge panels in the center of the ceiling. The frescoes continue to branch out until there was no way I could take in or grasp the entire montage. Not only was there more to see, but there was so much interaction, symmetry, spiritual and mystical significance, and metaphor. It was all too much.

Sir William Irwin Thompson wrote, "We are like flies crawling across the ceiling of the Sistine Chapel. We cannot see what angels and divinity lie underneath the threshold of our perceptions. We often do not live in the divine but we live in habituated perceptions. We live in an illusion that miracles are not possible."

My old vision of the Sistine Chapel being dominated only by the central picture of creation has been forever altered. The beauty remains, but the awe and infinite scope of the work and all it represents have taken the place of simple admiration.

"Ah, but I was so much older then…"

We are looking through a peephole and thinking it is the whole picture.

Paradoxically, the only way we can know the incompleteness of our vision is when our vision is expanded. That expansion can only occur when we have let go of our limited vision of the truth. It is only when we are not holding onto what we think we know that there is room for true knowing to enter.

Newcomers in Twelve Step recovery meetings will usually know more than anyone else, and are usually quick to let everyone know how intelligent they are. Gently they are reminded that "your best thinking got you here." Your best thinking landed you in a treatment center or at a meeting for people who are dealing with a serious addiction. In other words, "If you're so smart, how come you didn't figure out how to handle your problem all by yourself?" Some days our best thinking is not good enough.

Even though we might not know how we got into a particular difficult situation, our question needs to be, "What gets us out?" and the answer is, "The Power of God gets us out." Remember, the Power of God is also our power when we open ourselves to it. God's Power is our power when we are willing to surrender our ego, our self-will, into the greater, more powerful Will of God. The surrender into that Greater Presence brings with it love, peace, and joy.

When I am confronted with the deeper realities of living, I begin to realize no explanation is possible, and when I am in a peaceful spiritual place I realize no explanation is needed. When I am not peaceful, when I am trying to control, no explanation will be enough.

The thinking mind wants to explain, grasp, control, and put everything in neat little compartments; that is just what the mind does. So we seek out gurus, workshops, books, and all sorts of things that will give us the answer. Spirituality and the yearnings of our soul call us to go beyond our thinking mind, to go beyond our limited mental understanding, because there are many qualities and circumstances such as love, grace, peace, serenity, life, and death that we just cannot understand with our mortal mind.

The presence of God within us is constantly filling us with unconditional love, wisdom, healing, and much more. These blessings are happening all the time, and we participate in those gifts when we surrender. We let go into love; we let go into God; we let go of trying to grasp life; we let go of trying to understand it all with our thinking minds.

There is tremendous power in surrender; we let go of our little selves into the greatness of who we really are. We open ourselves to a power greater than our ego. We open ourselves to the infinite mystery of God.

Call to mind the image of Peter, seeing Jesus walking on the water, and Jesus holding His hand out saying, "Come." Peter takes his first faltering steps like an unsteady child. His eyes are only on Jesus, and Peter takes in the miraculous faith that Jesus' gaze brings. Then Peter's focus shifts and he begins to think, "What am I doing? I can't be doing this!" and with that thought, he sinks. (Mt 16:22-31)

Life is bigger than my mortal mind can grasp. Mortal means limited. It is not wrong, simply limited. There is nothing wrong with a bucket because it cannot hold the ocean.

Surrender is simply waking up to the truth of who you are: an unconditionally loved child of God. You would still have an ego, sort of a hat-rack to hang your varied roles in life on, but you would realize you are neither those roles nor the hat-rack, you are much more than that.

Because we do not see, we never fully appreciate what we behold. When Emily, in *Our Town* asked the stage manager if anyone really "got it," he answered, "Saints and poets, sometimes." Surrender makes us into saints and poets. It allows us to be receptive to all that is, free of judgment and free of fear.

In order to be more open to grace, I want to remind myself to remain as defenseless and unencumbered as possible. So much of why I experience myself as overwhelmed is that I keep such a tight hold on my fear and related feelings that they become like an angry cat–the tighter I hold, the more the cat fights so I have to hold on tighter. If I am holding the cat gently, as squirmy as he might be, he is much easier to handle and I will also be more at peace.

Although the results of surrender are infinite and immeasurable, some outcomes are obvious. Living in a mindful state of surrender is identical to living in a mindful state of the presence of God. Conscious surrender is the same as being enfolded within all the attributes of God, including peace, wisdom, love, and compassion. Living in surrender is living in the Now. Living in surrender does not eliminate the power of choice; it offers us unlimited freedom.

Does that mean we will never feel anything that is painful or difficult to deal with? No, of course not. We are still walking this human path, and even love sometimes means loss. Recall the tale of the grieving monk who explained to his disciples, "I am crying because I am sad." If you were to ask him, "Are you sorry that you loved your master so deeply?" through his tears of sadness, he would laugh at you! "What a ridiculous question," he would reply, "Of course I am not sorry I have loved." Will we feel loss, pain, and confusion sometimes? Of course, and we will also experience the exuberant flow of life.

I am not always in control of my feelings. There are some days when I will wake up and simply feel wonderful and energized. On those days I am like Teflon–nothing sticks to me. I am enfolded by my Observer consciousness, and am able to let go almost without a thought. The coffee spills; I am stuck in traffic. "Ah so." It is just all OK. Then there are other days, again with no particular reason, when even the sun shining through the window is annoying. Everything seems to go wrong. Instead of being Teflon, on days like that I am Velcro–everything sticks. In a state of surrender there will continue to be Teflon days and Velcro days, but I will not label them good or bad, they just are what they are. Some days will be up, some days will be down, but I will no longer be solely identified by my mood or circumstances. I will not be so affected by how the world appears to me on a certain day, because I would know the truth is deeper than any feeling or appearance.

Surrender is not simply altering my conscious thinking. In surrendering to the power of Spirit a new thinking arises from the God within. The old thinking was of the ego; the new is of Love. Although surrender is a spiritual process, my human actions remain important. I *choose* to consciously open myself up to God, to the flow of life, and all the other gifts that life in the Spirit bring, such as love, strength, wisdom, and serenity. When I do open myself to God, when I do surrender my self-will and my expectations, and act out of love and compassion, I am literally part of the Divine.

My openness to the flow of God, Grace, and Spirit is not measured or controlled by feelings or emotions. My feelings are as fickle as the weather. Some days I will feel close to God, others I will not. How I feel has nothing to do with how close God is. God is *always* close no matter how I feel.

"Energy follows thought" is a truth, but there is an even deeper truth. Prayer changes things. Love changes things. Opening yourself up, as best you can, to infinite love, grace, strength, abundance, and whatever else you might need is more powerful than any other thought you can have.

When something happens, do not ask, "Why is this happening to me?" That is the old guilt again. That is the old victim consciousness. Stop. The most loving approach to any situation of sickness or crisis is to prayerfully ask, "What can I do now?" or "What would love do?" Open yourself up to love and nurturing, not shame and blame. If your house were on fire, you would not stop to figure out, "Hmmmm, I wonder how that fire got started." How it got started is irrelevant. Put it out.

There was a holy picture that made the rounds years ago, of Jesus holding a lantern, knocking on the door of this little house where a pale frightened face peeped out one of the windows. The lesson for us was, "There is no handle on the outside of the door. Only you can let Jesus in." The image and message have merit, but they also can limit our vision.

It was not until much later in life I began to realize that we do not invite God in; God is already here. We do not make room for God in our lives; we consciously recognize God is already here. We can pretend God is not here. We can pretend we are not in the presence of unconditional love. We can pretend we are unlovable. This is what some teachers mean when they speak of this world as an illusion. On some level the world is real because I am writing this and you are reading this. The illusion is my thinking that I am separate from God.

I can choose to live in the illusion of separateness; I can live in the illusion that God is not with me or that God doesn't love me today, or God is not smiling on me. Those are the thoughts that create illusion. This is the truth: God is everywhere; God is love; you cannot help being touched by it. You can pretend you are not loved, but you always are.

Know God as the perfect expression of love, wisdom, strength, and compassion. When we are actively involved with those qualities of God, we are also *being* those qualities of the Divine. We are not just doing God's work, we are one with God. We are literally creating heaven on earth. Although we are always one with God, we participate in this Oneness when we are loving, compassionate, and wise. We participate in the Oneness of God when we are acting in concert with the qualities of God that are within us.

The mystery of surrender manifests in many ways. How many times has a miraculous piece of surrender shown up in my life such as a transformation of my thinking, and I have no way to explain it? In struggling with an addiction, how is it that one moment I am in denial and the next moment I am in acceptance and surrender? I cannot explain that.

There have also been times when I have worked and worked on surrendering something–like smoking, for example–and prayed, and did everything I knew how to do, and still I was smoking, until one day I wasn't. I certainly did not know that was the day I quit smoking, I just knew I did not smoke that day. I still had the craving, but it was not overpowering, and then I did not smoke the next day or the next. I cannot explain that either.

When I was working as a counselor and chaplain in treatment centers, I cannot tell you the number of times we would say, "Jane S. is doing so well, I really think she is going to make it," or "Joe J. is in so much denial, he doesn't even know he's being dishonest, he doesn't have a prayer." We were wrong about 95% of the time. Go figure.

When I was in treatment myself, my counselor and the staff had an exit interview with me, and they reported to me they had debated about keeping me there an extra week, but it was the consensus that it would do me no good. They did not think a week or a month or a year would allow them, or me, any more room for a breakthrough. They didn't say I was hopeless, but looking back I'm sure that's what they thought. Their parting words to me were, "We don't think you are going to make it." Well, honestly, neither did I. But guess what? Here I am. Thank you, God.

We all have incidents in our lives which have revealed mystery. We even realize some very painful times were times of very deep healing and transformation. How many times have we thought an event in our lives was a terrible thing, and looked back later and discovered how beautiful and important it was? Many times I will be wrestling with a life circumstance that defies explanation. I am usually angry about the pain and confusion, but after I have gotten to the other side, a client will come into the office with a similar situation happening with them, and here I sit with both the experience and some possible insights and solutions. Amazing!

Thomas Merton said, "We do not want to be beginners. But let us be convinced of the fact that we will never be anything but beginners, all our life!"

My beginning asserts itself in the prayer expounded by Emilie Cady, "God, I don't know the answer. You do. Show me."

Surrender is a mystery too big to be explained.

Love is a mystery; it is too big to be explained.

Embrace the mystery.

MEDITATION: MYSTERY

As you get comfortable, relaxed, and open, take a few deep cleansing breaths, opening even more.

Count backwards from ten to one as you breathe deeply. You can feel a sense of lightness and receptiveness as you allow Spirit to speak to you, sharing with you exactly what you need.

Breathe deeply and experience yourself more and more relaxed as you open to this meditation.

Breathe, let go, let go of all you think you are.

After all the surrenders are done, who is it that is left? Who surrenders?

Even as you ponder that question, notice there is a "you" who is looking at all the surrenders.

Imagine again you are floating in space, and you have in your hand a large transparent box.

Begin to put into this box all that you think you are. Throw in your physical form; then your past and anything in your past you might be clinging to; toss in your future which you cannot predict anyway. Throw in all the feelings and emotions connected with your past and future, guilt, shame, fear, worry, and doubt.

What would it be like to put all of your memories in the box? Put all your memories in the box, no matter what they are.

Hmmm. What else is left? All your addictions and attachments, throw them in. Throw in all the uniforms and all the roles you play in life.

Throw in that marvelous tool, your thinking mind. Throw your mind in the box. Throw in your dreams and ambitions, anything else you can think of, throw it all in.

Throw in your beliefs, everything you think you know, throw it all in.

And now let it go. Watch the box float away with all that you thought you were.

Whoever is left watching is much more who you are, even though it might not have a name or a form.

Now that you are completely unencumbered, breathe in the Oneness of God that is all around you and through you.

Breathe it in and know.

Work on keeping a conscious space between you and what you think you are.

Begin to be conscious again of your breathing. Breathe deeply and stretch. Come fully back here in your body, completely centered and grounded.

Get up, stretch, and look around you. Become familiar with the place again, feeling yourself in your body. Journal or process any other way you like.

NUGGETS

"God and I are one," we say, and immediately the mind pops in and says, "What, how can that be?"

"I don't know, but I know," the wise man once said. "I don't know with my mind but I know with my heart."

The first time we are called upon to surrender and to let go is quite frightening. Although the process becomes more familiar, there is never a point when we can say "Ah, that's it—I've got it." Spirituality is not something you get, it is something you do every day, sometimes every minute.

The mystery is that, through it all, it is still so beautiful.

Surrender into love because that is who you are.

You are here to remember you are divine but not to deny or reject your humanity.

I am so tired of trying to figure things out.

"I'm astounded by people who want to 'know' the universe when it's hard enough to find your way around Chinatown." –Woody Allen

Why would we hold onto anything that keeps us from love, truth, and peace?

We can know beyond our intellect. Both faith and intuition are modes of knowing. Faith is not some far-out religious thing. We use it all the time when we are crossing the street or obeying a traffic light.

Once I get it, I control it and I put it in a box or I pin it to a wall, but now it is dead, static, and lifeless.

If we are relaxed and open, knowing that we do not know, and in beginner's mind, then more is revealed to us which previously we did not know existed.

In surrender, we allow ourselves to be OK not knowing so we can understand more.

It might be an addiction, a loss, or a grieving we need to deal with, and we realize that all the thoughts and all the books in the world are not going to be enough to take care of this.

When we explore the power of the mind and the power of thoughts, keep this idea in mind: it is only when we know we are one with God that our words and thoughts carry the creative power of God.

Surrender is an illusion, but we have to do it anyway to realize what we are surrendering is an illusion as well as the surrendering itself. Nothing can separate us from the love of God.

REFERENCES

Anonymous, *Alcoholics Anonymous 3rd ed.* (New York: Alcoholics Anonymous World Services, Inc., 1976)

> Sometimes referred to as the "Big Book," this volume serves as a cornerstone for all recovery literature. Although some of the personal accounts in the second part of the book have been updated over the years, the first section, which describes the program of AA, has remained virtually untouched. A companion volume titled *The Twelve Steps and the Twelve Traditions* gives a more expanded and detailed view of the Twelve Steps of recovery.

Assagioli, Roberto, *Psychosynthesis* (New York: Penguin Books, 1976)

> This is a ground-breaking book which explores psychology and spirituality. Many substantive issues are followed up by the work of his student, Piero Ferucci. One of my favorite books is Ferucci's *Inevitable Grace*.

Buscaglia, Leo, *Love* (New York: Fawcett Crest, 1972)

> Leo was a wonderful author, but to get the full flavor of his energy you would have to hear him speak. *Love* is a beautiful little book. It might not define love for you, but it will tell you what it means.

Boylan, Gerry, *Christ in Training* (Louisville, KY: Chicago Spectrum Press, 2007)

> This is my first book, and I mention it here because it contains a deeper and more detailed description of how we initially become wrapped up in our ego-consciousness, and how we get out. There are also a number of ideas such as addiction, love, forgiveness, and non-judgment which are approached somewhat differently.

Cady, H. Emilie, *The Collected Works of Emilie Cady* (Unity Village, MO: Unity House, 1995)

> Consider this to be a classic in spiritual New Thought writing. Although her works were originally published in 1894, they remain totally relevant today. Ms. Cady has a profound grasp of scripture and uses it throughout her work to illumine and inspire.

Dass, Ram, *Still Here* (New York: Riverhead Books, 2000)

> I have only met Ram Dass twice on the physical plane, but for years he has been a teacher to me. His books and lectures continue to move and inspire me.

Fox, Emmet, *The Golden Key* (Unity Village, MO: Unity House, 1931)

> This pamphlet is a marvelous example that the most profound wisdom can also be

simply expressed. "Instead of focusing on the problem, turn your thoughts toward God." I would also encourage you to check out his classic work, *The Sermon on the Mount*.

Graham, Kenneth, *The Wind in the Willows* (New York: Aladdin Paperbacks, 1999)

A beautiful book meant for children and adults. It is a rare, wise, and whimsical story.

Kopp, Sheldon, *If You Meet the Buddha on the Road, Kill Him* (New York: Bantam, 1972)

Dr. Kopp was a New York psychiatrist. He writes with a marvelous depth of wisdom, humor, and self-honesty.

Kornfield, Jack, *A Path with Heart* (New York: Bantam Books, 1993)

Although this book is Buddhist in nature, it speaks to everyone on a spiritual path. It is full of practical wisdom, insight, and, most of all, love.

Merton, Thomas, *Thoughts in Solitude* (New York: Dell, 1961)

I never met Merton, but like other poets and pilgrims I have read, he became and remains a teacher to me. I think in part my attraction was the monk/Catholic connection, later it was the relationship with Buddhist ideas, today it is simply joining hands and hearts with a fellow traveler who is walking ahead of me.

Peck, M. Scott, *The Road Less Traveled* (New York: Simon and Shuster, 1978)

This book has been around for awhile. Its honesty and insights opened many doors for me to examine and grow with.

Seng-s'tan, *Hsin-Hsin Ming*, trans. Richard B. Clarke (Buffalo, NY: White Pine Press, 1970)

The *Hsin-Hsin Ming*, which is sometimes translated as *Verses in the Faith Mind*, is a poem written by Seng-s'tan, the third patriarch of Zen in the seventh century. It is one of the most beautiful and poignant pieces of literature I have encountered. I never tire of reading it or hearing it recited.

Schucman, Helen, and Thetford, William (scribes) *A Course in Miracles*, (Omaha, NE: Course in Miracles Society, 2006)

Originally scribed by Helen Schucman and William Thetford, both Professors of Medical Psychology at Columbia University's College of Physicians and Surgeons, *A Course in Miracles* is a work of spiritual psychology. It is actually three books: the Text; the Workbook: and the Manual for Teachers. A summation of the book's message is, "Nothing real can be threatened; nothing unreal exists; herein lies the peace of God."

There are a number of edits of this book, the version I am using is noted above. Personally I find it the easiest to read, and according to the editors it is the version which is closest to the original transcripts.

Small, Jacquelyn, *Transformers* (New York: Bantam, 1992)

> Jacquie is a wise woman, beloved teacher, and tireless seeker of the truth. We have a wonderful history dating back to 1982 when I first heard her speak. Shortly afterwards I attended one of her workshops on Psycho-Spiritual Integration. Her books, talks, and workshops continue to be a profound influence which continue to enhance my life.

> If you have the opportunity, attend one of her workshops or read one of her books, or even better do both.

Wilbur, Ken, *Grace and Grit* (Boston: Shambala, 1993)

> This is a beautiful and difficult book. Ken Wilbur, philosopher and poet, has taken on the task of synthesizing modern scientific thought, human history, psychology, and spirituality. This book is a vehicle for expressing many of his ideas, but it is also a compelling, heartfelt, heart-breaking, and heart-healing story of Ken and his wife Treya and her struggle with cancer.

All scripture references are from *The Good News Bible: The Bible in Today's English Version* (New York: Thomas Nelson, 1976) unless otherwise noted.